GLASNOST IN BRITAIN?

KV-577-738

Books are to be returned on or before
the last date below.

LIBREX —

LIVERPOOL POLYTECHNIC
LIBRARY SERVICE

TRUEMAN STREET LIBRARY

- 4 MAR 2003

295263/89.

LIBREX

3 1111 00210 3461

Buchan, N
Glasnost in Britain?: against censorship
T M 323.445 BUC 1989

Glasnost in Britain?

Against Censorship and in Defence of the Word

Edited by
Norman Buchan
and
Tricia Sumner

MACMILLAN

© Norman Buchan and Tricia Sumner 1989

All rights reserved. No reproduction, copy or transmission
of this publication may be made without written permission.

No paragraph of this publication may be reproduced, copied
or transmitted save with written permission or in accordance
with the provisions of the Copyright Act 1956 (as amended),
or under the terms of any licence permitting limited copying
issued by the Copyright Licensing Agency, 33–4 Alfred Place,
London WC1E 7DP.

Any person who does any unauthorised act in relation to
this publication may be liable to criminal prosecution and
civil claims for damages.

First published 1989

Published by
THE MACMILLAN PRESS LTD
Houndmills, Basingstoke, Hampshire RG21 2XS
and London
Companies and representatives
throughout the world

Typeset by Footnote Graphics,
Warminster, Wilts

Printed in Great Britain by
Camelot Press Ltd, Southampton

British Library Cataloguing in Publication Data
Glasnost in Britain?: against censorship and in defence of the
word.
1. Great Britain. Freedom of the press
I. Buchan, Norman II. Sumner, Tricia, *1947–*
323.44'5
ISBN 0–333–49057–6 (hardcover)
ISBN 0–333–49058–4 (paperback)

Contents

Contents

List of Tables

Preface

The Russians came to the 1987 Edinburgh Festival and brought their *glasnost* with them.

The major theme of the Festival was Russian music and theatre. But at the same time the Festival organised a conference to examine just what impact *glasnost* was making on the Soviet Union. The Deputy Soviet Cultural Minister, the Secretary of the Writers' Union and leading Soviet poets and writers (including the inevitable Yevtushenko) all participated. They were open. They were frank. Not only about what is happening in the present day Soviet Union but (even more startling to experienced Soviet watchers) about their painful history under Stalin – and after. Yevtushenko applauded when one of the present editors said that whether right or wrong Solzhenitsyn should be published in the Soviet Union. (As we go to press we learn that that is now going to happen.)

Something else happened. Paradoxically the conference made us sharply aware of how fast attitudes and environments were changing not only in their country but in ours too. As fast as the shades were going up in the Soviet Union they seemed to be coming down in Britain. This contrariety prompted Tribune, on the spur of the moment, to hold another conference a week later. This time to discuss the threat to the freedom of the word in Britain. What else could it be called but '*Glasnost* in Britain?'

This second conference inevitably covered a wide spectrum. In the earlier week we had been dealing with a single, tight, autocratic state censorship. In Britain the problem was varied, more varied than we knew. It was both direct and indirect, partly commercial, partly state interference, partly the classic conflict between the differing views of freedom – the social and the individual. Afterwards we realised how much in recent years had been happening to our accepted freedoms. We realised, too, that much more had still to be said.

We needed, in short, an anthology, each section written by someone authoritative in their own field and covering a wide range of the written and spoken word.

However diverse in background, profession or political and social views, those contributing have one thing in common.

They believe that, in recent years, censorship, direct and indirect, has increased, is increasing and ought to be diminished.

It is the theme of this book.

TRICIA SUMNER
NORMAN BUCHAN

Acknowledgement

The editors wish to thank Phyllida Shaw and the National Campaign for the Arts for giving permission to use the extract on theatre sponsorship from the article, 'Danger in the Wings', by Phyllida Shaw which appeared in the Spring 1988 issue of the *NCA News*.

T.S.
N.B.

Notes on the Contributors

Sir Kenneth Alexander is an economist who has spent most of his working life teaching, researching and administering in universities. He was formerly Chairman of Govan Shipbuilders and later Chairman of the Highland and Islands Development Board. From 1981 to 1986 he was Principal and Vice-Chancellor of the University of Stirling and in 1986 became Chancellor of the University of Aberdeen.

Tom Baistow is the author of *Fourth-Rate Estate: An Anatomy of Fleet Street*, and is well known as a commentator on the national press. He was formerly foreign editor of the *News Chronicle*, assistant editor of the *Daily Herald* and deputy editor of the *New Statesman*. As a reporter he has covered every kind of story from elections and strikes to the Congo war and the Olympic Games.

Steven Barnett is Head of Research at the Broadcasting Research Unit, an independent policy 'think tank' on the media. Having gained social science degrees from Cambridge University and the London School of Economics, he spent several years at the Consumers' Association, responsible for campaigning research on a wide range of consumer policy issues. He has written widely on broadcasting and communications.

John Benington is currently Director of the Local Government Centre at Warwick University. He has been a Lecturer in Policy Analysis and Management at the Institute of Local Government Studies, Birmingham University, Head of the Employment Department at Sheffield City Council and Director of the Home Office Community Development Project in Coventry. He is the co-author with Dr Judy White of *Leisure Services at a Crossroads* and is also co-editor with Dr Gerry Stoker of the journal *Local Government Policymaking*.

Michael Billington has been drama critic for the *Guardian* since 1971 and for *Country Life* since 1987. He also writes regularly about the London arts scene for the *New York Times* and *Vanity Fair*. He is a frequent broadcaster and has written and presented two extensive profiles for Channel 4 of Dame Peggy Ashcroft and Sir Peter Hall. His many books include *The Modern Actor*, studies of Alan Ayckbourn, Tom Stoppard and Ken Dodd, and, most recently, a biography of Peggy Ashcroft. In 1986 he was, under the chairmanship of Sir Kenneth Cork, a member of the team that carried out an enquiry into professional theatre in England.

Alistair Bonnington is a practising solicitor in Scotland and a partner in Bannatyne Kirkwood France & Co. in Glasgow. He specialises in advising newspapers and his firm is Scottish legal adviser to the publishers of the *Glasgow Herald* and *Evening Times*. He acts for Duncan Campbell in Scotland in connection with the proceedings taken against him by the Lord Advocate and for the *Glasgow Herald* in connection with the Cavendish case concerning the memoirs *Inside Intelligence*. He is an occasional contributor to newspapers and legal journals.

Norman Buchan, MP, has been a Labour MP since 1964, and now represents Paisley South. He was a Minister in two Labour Governments and has held several shadow positions including Arts and Media. He is a frequent contributor to political and cultural journals. He is the editor of *The Scottish Folksinger* and *101 Scottish Songs*. He is Vice President of the Poetry Society and Chairman of the *Tribune* Board.

Peter Fiddick has written about broadcasting for the *Guardian* as critic and commentator since 1970 and as Media Editor launched the first national newspaper media page in 1984. He writes the Research column for the *Listener*. A frequent broadcaster on media matters, he wrote and presented the ITV series *Looking at Television* and *The Television Programme*. He is co-author of the critical study *Enoch Powell on Immigration*.

Maurice Frankel is the Director of the Campaign for Freedom of Information, where he has worked since the Campaign was set up in January 1984. He previously worked for the corporate responsibility pressure group Social Audit and as a consultant to Friends of the Earth and is the author of several books on environmental pollution and occupational health and safety.

Phil Kelly has been editor of *Tribune* since March 1987, and has worked as a freelance journalist and public relations consultant, and been a staff member, contributor, or editorial collective member of several left and radical periodicals, including *7 Days*, *Time Out*, The *Leveller*, and *State Research*. He has been chair of the London Freelance Branch of the National Union of Journalists, and a Labour councillor in Islington.

John McGrath is a playwright, film and television writer, and director in all three, founder of 7:84 Theatre Companies in England and Scotland, and director of an independent film-producing company. He is the creator of 7:84's style of theatre for working-class audiences. His 36 plays include *The Cheviot, the Stag and the Black, Black Oil*, *Event While Guarding the Bofors Gun*, *Blood Red Roses*, etc. TV work includes early *Z-Cars* and films for Channel 4 including *The Reckoning* and *The Dressmaker*.

Murray Ritchie is assistant editor of the *Glasgow Herald*. He is principally a leader writer but also writes his Monday Column, which is news features, and he writes TV criticism. He was the first winner of the Fraser of Allander Scottish Journalist of the Year Award in 1980. He has subsequently won a variety of other press awards.

Heather Rogers is a barrister practising in London. She graduated in law from the London School of Economics and Political Science and is a Harmsworth Scholar of the Middle Temple and a Scarman Scholar of the Council of Legal Education.

Richard Shepherd, MP, has been Conservative MP for Aldridge-Brownhills since 1979. He introduced the Protection of Official Information Bill (Reform of Section 2 of the Official Secrets Act) which was defeated at Second Reading in the House of Commons on 15 January 1988. He has been a member of the Select Committee on Treasury and Civil Service since 1979.

Nigel Spearing, MP, has been a Labour MP since 1970, and now represents Newham South. He is known for his interest in and use of the procedures of the House and its practices. He has been a member of seven Select Committees, including Procedure and Foreign and Commonwealth Affairs. He is currently chairman of the Select Committee on EEC Legislation.

Lord Stockton is Chairman of Macmillan Publishers Ltd, and became the second Earl on the death of his grandfather in December 1986. After training with the *Glasgow Herald* and two years in Fleet Street with the *Daily Telegraph*, he was appointed Foreign Correspondent in Paris in 1967, eventually becoming Chief European Correspondent for the *Sunday Telegraph*. He joined the family publishers in 1970. In 1984 and 1985 he led the successful campaign in the United Kingdom against the imposition of VAT on knowledge. In 1988 he was active in representing the publishing trade in the Lords stage of the new copyright bill.

Dr Gerry Stoker is Lecturer in Public Administration at the Institute of Local Government Studies Birmingham University. He is author of *The Politics of Local Government* (Macmillan 1988) and co-author with Tim Brindley and Yvonne Rydin of *Remaking Planning*. He is also co-editor with John Benington of the Journal *Local Government Policymaking*.

Tricia Sumner is a political researcher at present working on arts and media policy. She was a Labour and Co-operative candidate at the 1987 general election. She was Secretary to the Labour Party Policy Committee on the Arts and Media.

1 *Glasnost* in Britain?
Norman Buchan and Tricia Sumner

The problem facing Gorbachev is immense. He is trying to lift the incubus of decades of a hard, cruel and oppressive state machine.

Whom men wish to control they first make silent. The system of control was buttressed by censorship and repression of the word. Never total: mankind is too complex – and courageous – for that. But a state structure, single and autocratic. Their problem is seen. It is known and sufficiently understood, however difficult it is proving for the liberal forces within the Soviet Union to alter.

Here it is different.

We have no single comprehensive state censorship. Yet we have reason to be anxious. The last decade of political life in Britain has been shot through with the use of secrecy and the consequences of secrecy. It has lead to sackings, resignations and trials. Britain today has become the most secretive of all the Western democracies. It is not however the obvious and now notorious political secrecy that gives rise to most concern, but that this has been accompanied by a network of other developments in a wider field where the freedom of the word and of thought is necessary, and is now alas at risk.

Who would have predicted ten years ago, for example, that a government proposal to end the century-old tradition of free public libraries would have passed virtually unchallenged? But that is what happened in February 1988. Victorian philanthropy was too advanced for the Britain of Mrs Thatcher's third term. Her 'Victorian Values' do not apparently extend to the literal 'freedom of the word'. The public silence about the Green Paper on Libraries[1] was worrying. It was almost a symbol as to how far and how fast we had already allowed market-place values to dominate our thinking. Some years ago in a radio programme, referring to Victorian philanthropy, Marghanita Laski asked us to imagine that free public libraries had never existed. What would happen, she asked, if a local council suddenly announced that they had an idea: they had decided to use the rates to construct a building, line it with shelves and fill it with books, all to be loaned free to the community. What shock would be created! What spendthrift nonsense! She underestimated the degree of regression. She did not envisage that a future government would as a matter of conscious policy begin to reverse the accepted good of the free library system.

If Laski had warned, then Lord Gowrie predicted. As Minister for Arts and Libraries during the second Thatcher term (24 September 1984) he opened a library in Ealing. The Office of Arts and Libraries was sufficiently pleased with what he had to say that an official press release was issued. Gowrie said that he was pleased that they were introducing charging, because, he added:

> If a charge is made . . . then the user will appreciate what he or she is getting, use will be restricted to those who really have an interest, rather than a whim, and extra resources are available for the service as a whole. I suggest that a well run library authority should always raise a charge if it is legally entitled to do so.

It was a neat encapsulation of the free market philosophy. Things will be appreciated more if you pay for them (the philosophy of the harlot through the ages!); people will not be allowed to drop in to cultural centres simply on a whim – though that fortuitous step is how almost every person has first developed an interest in books, or anything else; and finally money will cross the counter to keep down the rates.

But to be fair to Lord Gowrie, he *did* say that he was opposed to charging for the loan of books. (Though, regrettably, not because it was wrong, but because it would be illegal.) Within four years events had bypassed even monetarist Gowrie. His successor, Richard Luce, Minister of Arts and Libraries in a Thatcher third term, deals briskly with Gowrie's problem about illegality. He simply proposes to change the law to allow charging for books.

This is not a minor matter. For over a century, and for very good reason, the central tenet of public library legislation has been that books should be free, that a library is a community resource of knowledge, and that access to such knowledge should be a right and a freedom unrestricted by an individual's ability to pay.

The Library Green Paper is one of a series of three green papers, all of which emphasise 'financing' – two of them include the word 'Financing' in their title – rather than how to provide an efficient and developing service. Each of these green papers constitutes an attack upon our culture, and specifically an attack on freedom of expression and access to knowledge within that culture.

Perhaps the most immediately significant of these three green papers is the Peacock Report on Broadcasting.[2] It disturbs because it simply surrenders to technology. It simply assumes that since we cannot control satellite broadcasting by existing regulatory methods, then we should lie back, close our eyes and think of England! From this premise it goes on to argue that broadcasting should be allowed to follow the pattern of the development of the 'free press' since the ending of pre-censorship in 1694. This development has of course ended in a situation where three people, Maxwell, Murdoch and Stevens, control 80 per cent of the popular press in this country.

Tragically, the Peacock Committee themselves recognised what the parallel consequence of this free market broadcasting would be: an inevitable destruction of the basic existing duty of all broadcasting in Britain to 'inform, educate and entertain' and its replacement by some of the worst programme inadequacies that we have seen in 'free' television elsewhere (see Table 3.1 on p.31). Because they recognised this they proposed in compensation to create a kind of cultural ghetto to be called 'public patronage'. They make clear what they expect to be missing from the generality of television pro- grammes under their proposals. These omissions would therefore have to be included within this – by definition, underfunded – patronage system. They say: 'Four key words we would suggest here are knowledge, culture, criticism and experiment.'

Most people would regard that extraordinary sentence as covering a pretty big area for a minor ghetto. And they would be right. The Committee go on to specify:

(i) There should be news, current affairs, documentaries, pro- grammes about science, nature and other parts of the world, as well as avowedly educational programmes, all of which require active and not passive attention and which may also contribute to responsible citizenship.
(ii) There should be high quality programmes on the Arts (music, drama, literature, etc.) covering not only performance but also presentation of and comment on the process of artistic creation.
(iii) There should be critical and controversial programmes, covering everything from the appraisal of commercial products to politics, ideology, philosophy and religion.[3]

After reading that list one might well ask what is left of good broadcasting. The answer must be 'very little' and yet that 'very little' is what the Report must regard as the future pattern of the generality of British television. Not least of the problems of such an approach is that the creation of majority audiences for new type programmes would be inhibited. Despite what Lord Gowrie says, majority audiences *can* be built up through an accidental viewing or a whim. Who, for example, could have predicted mass audiences watching bats in a cave or insects in British grasses, but Attenborough and Bellamy, by being given an opportunity outside a ghetto in the mainstream of public service broadcasting, have achieved just that. Yet these programmes have been among the glories of British television and their crucial importance in relation to freedom of access and the expansion of knowledge is obvious. By relegating them to a kind of specialised interest enclosure, immediate barriers are established to access and knowledge.

The third green paper is on radio.[4] This one specifically removes the obligation to 'inform, educate and entertain' from their proposed new commercial national and local stations. Instead these will be 'more lightly regulated'. It poses the incredible question: 'Is it still realistic for all radio at all levels to have to be of high quality ...?' But this of course is precisely a prescription for low quality broadcasting, whether in so-called serious programmes, popular music, comedy, news or anything else. Indeed, the Government recognises this consequence but dismisses it for the whole of the huge commercial radio network they are proposing to establish. For this 'a lighter system of regulation would omit the ... positive obligations to attain high standards of quality and range.' Quite cold-bloodedly they are prepared to set up a new and massive broadcasting structure solely for commercial and profit making purposes. They recognise in advance that it will be inferior, and excuse themselves by throwing the burden of provision onto the remaining public sector. There the BBC 'should continue to provide programmes of high quality, comprising information, education and entertainment and of wide range and diversity.' However, they see no reason why the BBC should need all their present frequencies to be used to perform this pretty basic task! Therefore, they argue, these 'frequencies assigned to it [the BBC] could be better used to allow new national radio services provided on commercial lines.'

After all this they end with the bland comment:

> Given the assurance of quality which the continuation of BBC services will provide, there is no reason to build any statutory expectations that new services must between them provide programmes of comparable weight and mix.

These three papers put together, quite apart from their cultural implications, constitute a massive threat to the freedom of the word –

written and spoken. Unquestionably, libraries, radio and television have been a major source for the dissemination of information and ideas, for instruction, for education. Their limitation means a major contraction in the dissemination of thought. The bread and circuses concept that has been developed in the two green papers on broadcasting is almost a contemptuous retreat to a kind of helot based society. When the paper on radio casually dismisses 'range and diversity' they are by definition limiting the broadcasting of views to a narrow, competitive range, not in excellence or diversity, but with the main aim of maximising audiences at all possible times. And that is of course best achieved by programmes which are least likely to irritate, or stimulate, or antagonise by being provocative, experimental, or merely different. This restricted range inevitably sets a restricted agenda for thought. It is the censorship of limitation.

Tragically, a new and developing concept in broadcasting, which had the opportunity of widening the agenda, involving people as producers and not only as consumers of the word, through the medium of community radio, has also been rejected. This, too, it seems will be transformed into local commercial 'pop' programmes. It is a particularly sad setback for the ethnic communities who had visualised this as an important means of speaking to one another within their own community and also in broadcasting their community's views and culture more widely to the society of Britain as a whole.

Hitherto the regulated nature of British broadcasting has protected diversity of opinion and a comparative freedom of expression along a wide range of views, whatever might have been happening in the press. Indeed, even 30 or 40 years ago there might have been some validity in Peacock's comment about moving broadcasting towards the same pattern as the 'free' press. There was the *Daily Mirror* with its brilliant, popular journalism – radical, socially concerned and iconoclastic. There was the *Daily Express* front-paging foreign affairs and developing the idiosyncratic views of Lord Beaverbrook. There was, in short, a seriousness of purpose and a diversity of opinion within the popular press. Not so now. With the triple monopoly (a tripoli?) these have now become basically commodities for sale, a form of magazine, concerned largely with stories (real or imaginary) about pop stars, soap operas and the Royal Family. There is nothing wrong with that – but there is something wrong with *only* that. Above all, there is something even more wrong with only that if broadcasting too is to move in that direction. What is claimed to be providing an expanding choice is in fact limiting choice.

In a curious way the presence, side by side, of a regulated broadcasting system and a 'free press' epitomises the argument about the nature of freedom. In broadcasting the imposition of regulation ensured sufficient diversity of programme and opinion to allow freedom of the word at large, both to the consumer and to the producer. Paradoxically, the total freedom of the newspaper proprietor has ended with lack of freedom of choice and therefore a lack of freedom of the word, for both the producer – the journalist – and the consumer.

But now with the move towards deregulation in broadcasting, following the pattern of the contemporary press (and, incidentally, the same ownership!), there will be no regulated assurance of choice remaining in either broadcasting or the popular press. The lack of choice in one reinforces the lack of choice in the other. Effective lack of choice in terms of concepts and ideas is almost of itself a definition of censorship.

These three green papers all propose changes in structure, conceived in the name of freedom and not primarily designed deliberately and directly to censor. Censorship here is an unhappy but inevitable side product of the drive towards profit and the free market. But there has been a more directly sinister development taking place in Thatcher's third term and that is the move towards a conscious censorship, a thematic censorship. Like the green papers, this too is a threefold threat.

The most unpleasant of the three is Section 28 introduced by backbench Tory MPs in Committee at a late stage of the Local Government Act. It reads:

A local authority shall not –
(a) intentionally promote homosexuality or publish material with the intention of promoting homosexuality;
(b) promote the teaching in any maintained school of the acceptability of homosexuality as a pretended family relationship.

Neither frontbench had sufficient courage immediately to reject it. Inevitably, from that point on it was defined and redefined by a succession of Ministers as they attempted to allay some of the arguments and fears that it aroused. The difficulty remains; it is not what Ministers say, it is what the Act says that matters and how far it will extend will not be known unless and until a case arises.

Already warning advice is being given in local authorities, instructing teachers to be careful. Librarians are anxious as to how far this prohibition might extend to books on their shelves. Oscar Wilde has been mentioned, André Gide has been mentioned. Theatres receiving local authority grants have been warned. If the sonnets of Shakespeare have not been mentioned, then they should be!

Since Section 28 was introduced at a late stage and in a hurry and perhaps in the wrong Act, curious things arise. In education it applies only to local government schools. Presumably, said someone at a later stage in the House of Commons, in Eton or Harrow we can let joy by unconfined!

It is doubtful whether the Section was ever introduced to deal with the specific of 'the intentional promotion of homosexuality'. That was never a problem, either in school or in library. Its intention was to change the public perception of homosexuality and homosexuals, to reverse the mood of the liberalising 1967 Act. Above all it was meant to censor. We may never get a legal judgment on it for the Section was not designed to ensure the bringing of such a case. It was designed to inhibit and intimidate. The purpose of censorship is to prevent not to punish – that is its strength and its danger. This nasty little law shares that purpose.

And so too do the other two elements of this thematic censorship. Only Section 28 has so far become law. Of the others, one, the Broadcasting Standards Council, has been introduced without a law being passed and the other (Gerald Howarth's Obscene Publications Bill) failed as a Private Member's Bill in 1987 due to the approaching election. This had been the second such Bill of that term of Parliament. The first was introduced by Winston Churchill. This contained a horrendous 'laundry list' of acts to be deemed obscene. Unfortunately, this list would, among other things, have eliminated half of Greek mythology! It ran into the ground after he had totally changed it on three separate occasions.

Howarth took a different tack. His main aim was to attack television and he extended the Obscenity Act to it. In the process he sought to redefine 'obscenity'. It was a difficult task, and certainly too difficult for him. It had foxed learned counsel and distinguished judges over the years and in few cases had those prosecuting emerged with very much dignity. Still fresh in people's minds was the trial for obscenity of '*Lady Chatterley's Lover*' when the prosecutor, Mervyn Griffith-Jones – in the 1960s of all decades – could pose the question to the jury: 'Is it a book that you would even wish your wife or your servants to read?' (Quite apart from the servants, certainly at least the three female jurors did not possess wives!) Curiously the trial had the same effect as the *Spycatcher* trials – it made people want to read the book! It resembled *Spycatcher* in another way too – in both cases the prosecution ended up looking extremely foolish.

Regrettably, Mr Howarth did too. In seeking to amend the 1959 Obscene Publications Act he got himself rather trapped in definitions. His problem was that the 1959 Act referred to 'articles'. When asked what this meant he said: 'Oh, items of bondage'. And for the next few columns of *Hansard* he got himself tied up, as it were, in 'bondage'. No one had the opportunity to tell him that 'articles' were already defined in the parent Act as 'any matter to be read or looked at or both, any sound record, and any film or other record of a picture or pictures.' Not being sure of what he was talking about, it is not surprising that his attempt to amend the basic definition in his Bill came unstuck, too. He redefined obscenity as those things which 'a reasonable person would regard as grossly offensive'. The trouble with that is that it contained three indefinables, especially indefinable in this field – 'reasonable', 'offensive' and, perhaps above all, 'grossly'. This last begs the question: how long is a piece of string?

Though happily the Bill fell, Mrs Thatcher promised that the Government itself would bring it back. This was re-affirmed on page 70 of the 1987 Conservative Party Manifesto, *The Next Moves Forward*. Despite this promise and perhaps fearful of past failures of legislation in this area, she has produced without consultation, and apparently without consideration, yet a third element of censorship. With her proposed Broadcasting Standards Council under the Chairmanship of Lord Rees-Mogg as Grand Censor she has gone back to the discredited notion of the Lord Chamberlain. Like the proposed legislation on obscenity its remit will be to deal with sex and violence.

But, as always with this type of legislation and with the type of people who propose it, it is the *serious* treatment of sex and violence which is attacked. During the Howarth Bill, alongside bondage, the proposers of the Bill kept coming back time after time to attack one production, *The Singing Detective*, a play which has won golden opinions throughout the world. It looks as though we now have a battle, which we thought was won long ago.

In 1907 Bernard Shaw listed the plays banned by the Lord Chamberlain in his time. It included *Mrs. Warren's Profession* by Shaw himself; *Waste* by Granville Barker; Ibsen's *Ghosts*; Shelley's *The Cenci*; *La Dame aux Camélias* by Dumas, and for good measure *Oedipus Rex* and that sombre masterpiece by Tolstoi, *The Power of Darkness*.

In a typically brilliant letter to *The Nation* (11 November 1907) Bernard Shaw attacked the main weakness of censorship: it bans the serious and fosters the sleazy:

And there you have the effect of the censorship in a nutshell. It does not forbid vice; it only insists that it shall be made attractive. It does not forbid you to put the brothel on the stage; it only compels you to advertise its charms and suppress its penalties. Now it is futile to plead that the stage is not the proper place for the representation and discussion of illegal operations [that is, abortion], incest and venereal disease. If the stage is the proper place for the exhibition and discussion of seduction, adultery, promiscuity and prostitution, it must be thrown open to all the consequences of these things or it will demoralise the nation. Either prohibit both or allow both. The censorship admits that it cannot do both. To do that would be to wipe the theatre out of existence . . . [so] it buys off the licentious playwrights and managers by licensing their agreeable plays and suppresses the stern, public-spirited and intellectually honest writers who insist on drawing the moral.

Like himself and Sophocles and Ibsen, he might have added.

It was not surprising therefore that the successor to the Lord Chamberlain, Rees-Mogg, cited as his current favourite programme *'Allo 'Allo*. This, which had started as a genuine satire of an earlier television series on the French Resistance, is now silly, sleazy, titillating. It treats sex, sadism and bondage as light farce. Bernard Shaw had it right in his analysis of a Lord Chamberlain!

Recalling the partly stimulated reaction against *Tumbledown* – the attacks by Tory MPs, their echo in some of the popular press – it must be a matter for doubt as to whether *Tumbledown* would have been shown had the Broadcasting Standards Council been in full operation. We have a historical parallel. In 1916 Miles Malleson wrote a play *Black 'Ell*. In it a soldier returns from the front. He has killed six Germans, the last with a knife – as with the broken bayonet in *Tumbledown*. He is welcomed as a hero, but, horrified by what he has done, cannot purge his memory of it. As the crowd gathers outside to cheer him he says:

We have had enough. The men in the trenches have had enough . . . I am not going back . . . I am going to stop at home and say it is all mad . . . I am going to keep on saying it . . . somebody's got to get sane again . . . I won't go back . . . I won't, I won't . . .

As the curtain falls on him, the crowd outside, unknowing, are still cheering.

There was then a Lord Chamberlain. There was the practice of censorship. The play was seized and was not performed until after the war. But at least then there had been the excuse of war. It was performed six years after his war – as was *Tumbledown* after the Falklands – but without fuss or hysteria.

The danger we are facing with this 'thematic' censorship is not that it will necessarily lead to a proliferation of court cases. What it does is much worse. It sows doubts and anxieties in the mind of writers, producers, directors. It establishes the practice of heavy self-censorship. Production costs are heavy; producers must play safe. Given an established Broadcasting Standards Council and a *de facto* Lord Chamberlain *Tumbledown* might never have been written – or produced. The same thing is true of the proposed obscenity law and of Section 28. Self-censorship is even more dangerous than overt censorship for it never sees the light of day. We do not know the totality of its effects. Too much never reaches the production stage. We have seen this beginning to happen in broadcasting after *Real Lives* and *Zircon*. For example, a *Panorama* programme on *Spycatcher* was voluntarily withdrawn after ten weeks of preparation.

Self-censorship is in any case self-defeating. It merely lowers the threshold at which the next direct intervention begins.

All this is especially serious because, whereas the Lord Chamberlain censored only the theatre, the Broadcasting Standards Council, we are told, will extend its range to violence in current affairs, news and documentaries. One of the most memorable and violent pictures in many people's mind is that of the small Vietnamese child, burning with napalm, running down the road towards the camera. It was right to show it. Images like that helped to end that war.

This extension to news and comment, therefore, adds a new dimension even to the traditional censorship. Writing in 1970, Richard Findlater in *Comic Cuts – Censorship in Action* said that censorship in Britain is commonly identified as being concerned with sex or 'dirty words'.

> No censorial controversies are aroused by most of the erstwhile deadly sins: ... Only Lust retains its power to disturb the state and its censors ... Gluttony, Avarice, Pride, Anger and Envy are, indeed, encouraged and sponsored in the consumer society.

These sins have since been turned into the positive virtues of a

Thatcher Britain. Much of the media, too, has been sucked into this ethos.

At the time of *Comic Cuts* the resurrection of the whole discredited paraphernalia of censorship was not on the agenda. We could take a fairly relaxed attitude to the history of the censor. However reactionary they might have been they were almost always at the same time absurd. The Lord Chamberlain's intervention on Theatre Workshop's *Fings Ain't Wot They Used T'Be* for example:

> The builder's labourer is not to carry the plank of wood in the erotic place and at the erotic angle that he does, and the Lord Chamberlain wishes to be informed of the manner in which the plank is in future to be carried.

George Devine at the Royal Court Theatre was also asked to make changes in Samuel Beckett's *End-Game*:

> *page 17*: For: 'I'd like to pee.'
>   substitute: 'I'd like to relieve myself.'
> *page 24*: For: 'What about that pee?'
>   substitute: 'What about that relieving yourself.'[5]

Since then an easy and casual restoration of censorship has slipped onto the wider stage. Secrecy has become almost another arm of government, and the consequences have affected all the media of communication. Because of secrecy, news can be manipulated. Lobby briefings, unattributed, are used to divert or conceal or to direct thinking. The 'unattributable' quote has become a way of life at the expense of the public right to know. The Chief Press Officer of No.10 has become a major political figure. The inadequacies of the popular press, and often a willing or easy subservience to the present regime, reinforce the power of central government in its ability to censor directly or indirectly. So much and so rapidly has this acceptance of secrecy affected us that we had at one time judges considering putting a ban on the reporting of Parliamentary exchanges about *Spycatcher*: at another point the Speaker ruling that because the matter was before the courts aspects of *Spycatcher* could not be discussed in the House of Commons.

Hitherto we have regarded the sovereignty of Parliament as a sufficient democratic defence. We have had a Secrecy Act, therefore, but no Freedom of Information Act. But what we are now witnessing is not so much the sovereignty of Parliament as the sovereignty of the Executive. In this narrow exclusive world the assumption is that theirs is the right to information as theirs is the right to power. Intervention comes casual and easy. With such an attitude they find it difficult to understand why people should question their actions. And, when people do question, the Executive is prepared to throw the whole apparatus of the state against them. What was astonishing about the whole *Spycatcher* saga was that any government could be so obsessed with its own right to secrecy that it was prepared to allow the world wide humiliation of its most senior civil servant – and either prepared to tolerate, or failed to understand, the ridicule this had brought upon themselves.

After all *Spycatcher* had at least been saying serious things: the subversion of a government happens to be a fairly serious matter! If the purpose was to conceal this the Government was going a strange way about it. If the charge of subversion was worth pursuing, it should have been pursued in the form of an enquiry. If it were not, then the whole farce and mockery of the episode was not worth the effort, time and money spent on it. In fact *Spycatcher* as a book was not really very important. What was important was that the legal case, and the publicity surrounding it, brought together and exposed, for those who wished to see, what had been happening in the whole field of expression and freedom of communication.

It involved the suppression of the written word in a book. It involved the suppression of the written word in the press. It involved suppression of reporting in broadcasting. It involved suppression of the spoken and written word within Parliament. It involved the use of the courts to suppress. In relation to *Spycatcher* alone it might not have mattered so very much. In relation to what was happening to our freedoms it was a crucially important signal.

During the same period in the USA we witnessed 'Irangate'. A highly secret and totally improper government action was exposed by witnesses testifying under oath. It was broadcast live throughout their country. Irangate might not have happened in Britain. But, if it had, it is doubtful if it would have been exposed. In America they have some access to the truth as of right and by law, however painful some of the proceedings may be. In the Soviet Union they are painfully trying to unscramble an apparatus of secrecy. In Britain we have failed even to transform in any substantial way the totally discredited Secrecy Act. (See chapters 8 and 9.)

Two factors help to underpin the secretive state. One is the twin use by government of the Official Secrets Act and, when it fails, the law of confidence against the 'honest whistle-blower', whom their own over-secretive methods have helped to create (see chapter 11). The other is the question of libel. This, too, is a doubly unjust factor. It is heavily weighted on the side of the rich and powerful. The threat of an expensive libel case can deter a necessary publication – or even cause destruction of a publication, as we have seen in the case of a recent biography. On the other hand it can equally deter the just but poor from suing.

There is no question but that the threat of a libel case coming from powerful sources can, and does, deter often fair and accurate comment. This is especially so in the case of books. Popular newspapers can carry a costly action and survive, as has been shown, for example, in the expensive Jeffrey Archer case. In addition the newspaper will already have recouped some of the financial costs in publicity and increased sales. A book publisher, however, might find their total investment lost as well as heavy libel costs if the case goes against them, but again it is the fear rather than the actuality of the costs which acts as an advance self-censorship of the word.

Similarly the triple monopoly in the press is no layer balanced by a confident, publicly responsible broadcasting system. On the contrary it is one under continual pressure and about to be changed to the same commercial control as the press.

There is little constitutional right of access to the most basic of information. The sovereignty of Parliament as a democratic doctrine pre-supposes an ease of response to the need to extend democratic freedom and extend liberties. It is not enough. Our freedoms must now be protected and enshrined through direct legislation; witnesses before Select Committees put under oath where necessary; a Freedom of Information Act; the right of access to all computerised information about ourselves; the Right of Reply; a replacement of the costly libel framework by an easier, cheaper and more open system of redress.

It is the total combination we have to fear: the commercial monopoly in the press and now forecast for radio and television, and the increasing governmental intervention in the media, in academic work, in local democracy. It is all the more dangerous because less obvious than an open state control.

Tragically our government has also developed around it a kind of crude anti-intellectual philistinism. When Duncan Campbell's flat was being 'visited' by the Special Branch the television cameras were out in force. As a window of his home appeared on the screen a voice-over accusingly said 'We can clearly see his room lined with shelves of books'. It was meant as an indictment. We have moved a long way not just from Marghanita Laski but sadly from the improving zeal of the Victorians.

The Soviet Union still has a long, long way to go but there is an uneasy feeling that as they are on the long climb up from the valley in their slow cablecar they may soon be passing us on our rapid and slippery way down.

Adam Czerniawski, the contemporary Polish poet, writing in a collection of modern Polish poetry called *The Burning Forest*, says of their struggle:

> No, our refusal, dissent and obduracy
> Didn't require great character.
> We had a pinch of indispensable courage
> – but basically it was a matter of taste.

Glasnost in Britain? It surely cannot be so difficult for us!

Acknowledgements

We are grateful for the assistance of the British Theatre Association and the Theatre Museum Library for their assistance in tracking down information about the Miles Malleson play *Black 'Ell*.

Our thanks, too, to Jozef Głogowski for drawing our attention to the quotation from *The Burning Forest* and to Bloodaxe Press for permission to use it.

Notes

1. Financing our Public Library Service: Four Subjects for Debate (Cm.324)
2. Report of the Committee on Financing the BBC (Cmnd.9824) (Technically not a 'Green Paper'.)
3. *ibid*. Paragraph 563
4. Radio: Choices and Opportunities (Cm.92)
5. Richard Findlater: *Comic Cuts – A bedside sampler of censorship in action.*

2 Broadcasting: A Catalogue of Confrontation

Peter Fiddick

It is not necessary to have a conspiracy theory, or even a particularly strong political viewpoint, to find something deeply troubling in the relationship between government and broadcasters in a period which has seen – *inter alia* – one Cabinet Minister threaten to use his powers to have a programme banned, another call for one not to be transmitted, a third carry on a sustained campaign against one broadcaster's news coverage, and pictures of Special Branch police officers confiscating videotapes from a studio.

At the very least, one might suspect that old conventions are breaking down – perhaps because politicians are wishing to extend their powers? Perhaps because broadcasters are encroaching on new territories? At worst, it might be suggested that these occurrences, and more besides, are manifestations of an ideological cast that sees the media not as the Fourth Estate but as tools of government. The fact that politicians involved might individually and sincerely deny having such intentions would not necessarily be proof that it was not so: there might still be room for suggesting, in this area of policy as in some others, that individuals did not realise what government collectively was doing.

I am by inclination not a conspiracy theorist. Too much in this world is explicable by what journalists tend to call the cock-up theory of the media, and there are examples enough of that, too, in the matters under consideration here.

Nevertheless, the catalogue of confrontations between government and broadcasters, and especially the BBC, in the relatively brief period since 1985 makes salutary reading. It has to be seen as a time of unique pressure against broadcast journalism in particular, the more disturbing for coinciding with the parallel government-sponsored pressure on broadcasting's economic base as typified by the Peacock Report and the ensuing debate about both the BBC licence fee and the ITV companies' franchises. There have been many times of friction between broadcasters and politicians, of all hues, and there is a case for saying that this is the way it should be, but in the 30-odd

15

years since television became a major mass medium in Britain, there has been no period like this.

The main events in the sequence are almost all connected with the BBC programmes.

First, in the summer of 1985, a documentary programme called *The Edge of the Union*, one of a series called *Real Lives*, was denounced for featuring, as one of two Northern Irish faction leaders of extreme and conflicting views, a leading IRA figure, Martin MacGuinness. In what became known as 'The *Real Lives* Affair', the Home Secretary called upon the governors of the BBC to withdraw the programme, threatening to use his own powers if they did not. A serious rift was exposed between the governors and senior BBC management, and on one day there was a protest strike by journalists which was joined by non-BBC workers and by those working for the BBC External Services. The ripples spread worldwide.

In April 1986, United States Air Force aircraft based in Britain bombed targets in Libya in reprisal for terrorist attacks on Americans that had been backed, or were alleged to have been backed, by the Gadafi regime. Debate surrounding this deeply controversial event itself quickly turned to charges from the British government party that the BBC's coverage of it had been biased, complaints which simmered through the summer until Mr Norman Tebbit, then chairman of the Conservative Party, told its annual conference that this was to be the focus of a detailed study of BBC television news a party group had been preparing. Finally delivered on 30 October – though pointedly published first through the rival news organisation, ITN – the document led to a detailed rebuttal from the BBC followed by long-drawn out sporadic sniping from Mr Tebbit which eventually seemed to embarrass even his senior colleagues, and was terminated towards the end of the year only by a sharp letter from the BBC's new chairman, Mr Marmaduke Hussey.

But through this period the two sides were also embroiled in two quite different and scarcely less noisily contested issues. One of them might appear not to fall strictly in this category of government pressure, since it involved a libel case brought personally by two Conservative backbench MPs against the current affairs programme *Panorama*. Nevertheless, the programme, entitled 'Maggie's Militant Tendency', broadcast more than two years earlier on 30 January 1984, had concerned charges of connections between Conservative politicians and extreme right-wing groups and, in its immediate aftermath, representations to the BBC were led by the then Chairman of the Party, John Selwyn Gummer, and the Conservative Chief

Whip, John Wakeham. In October 1986, when the BBC's governors had forced the management to settle out of court after a few days of hearings during which only the plaintiffs' side had been heard, a hundred Tory MPs signed a motion calling for the resignation of the Director General, Alasdair Milne. The case certainly had a significant place in what was now becoming a complex set of pressures between politicians, broadcasting authority, and – not quite the same thing – broadcast journalists.

Simultaneously, a new issue was developing. In late August 1986 BBC television held a perfectly routine press conference to introduce the BBC2 autumn programme schedule. It included mention of a new documentary series called *Secret Society* which would cover a number of aspects of secrecy in Britain, ranging from the work of Cabinet Committees and loopholes in the Data Protection Act to government contingency preparations for war and a rather vague reference to communications satellites. It drew a certain amount of press attention because of the indications that restricted information would be disclosed and because the freelance journalist at the centre of the series was Duncan Campbell, well known for his investigative work on similar issues in the left-wing magazine, *New Statesman*. These press reports, in turn, attracted the attention of the Ministry of Defence official who was secretary of the D-Notice Committee, a long established though uneasy joint MOD and media operation which serves as a semi-formal conduit for warning the media when matters of national security might be involved.

BBC executives, including the Deputy Director General, Alan Protheroe, who had oversight of the corporation's journalism and Pat Chalmers, the Controller of BBC Scotland through which the series was being produced, were well apprised of its possible sensitivity and its progress was being quite closely monitored – albeit with the complication of the production's physical distance from the centre of the organisation. After the initial publicity, and through the autumn, it was under even closer scrutiny, which resulted in December in a decision by Milne and his board of management to show five of the films but not the sixth, now known by the name of the spy satellite project on which it centred, *Zircon*.

The Christmas holiday period intervened. Then, in mid-January, the production team having learnt of the decision, the story broke in the press. Duncan Campbell said he would show the film to MPs, the BBC warned its staff not to, but within two days the Treasury solicitors had moved. Injunctions were taken out against Campbell, and there followed the remarkable sight of Special Branch men ransacking first Campbell's London home, and then making an unheralded weekend visit to the offices of BBC Glasgow, whence they carted off piles of written material and every foot of film relating to the series. Recorded by the BBC's own news cameras, here was more footage that went around the world, carrying a vivid message that relations between the British authorities and the world's archetypal public service broadcasting organisation were not what might have been supposed.

There was more to come. Attention in 1987 shifted to the *Spycatcher* affair, the government's efforts to ban publication of the memoirs of former intelligence officer Peter Wright. It was to prove one of the longest (and, it has to be said, most entertaining) legal wrangles in the entire period. It raised central issues (treated elsewhere in this book) and its direct focus was on the press. But it was in this context that an apparently innocuous BBC radio series called *My Country Right or Wrong*, which had interviews with other intelligence people, was suddenly propelled into the area of official displeasure and legal threats against which the corporation was obliged to defend it.

If the BBC was to bear the brunt of this litany of pressure and complaint, for whatever reasons, it was not alone. In mid-1988, when things seemed to have gone a touch quieter on the broadcasting front, an ITV programme, in Thames Television's *This Week* current affairs strand, was publicised as being about to raise questions concerning the killing in Gibraltar of three IRA members. They were suspected of having planted a car bomb – they hadn't, it soon transpired, but it was acknowledged that they intended to – by a British SAS squad who had been whipped in and out of the Rock for their interception mission. Several weeks on, *This Week* had come up with eye witnesses to the shooting who cast doubt on the necessity for the killings.

Three years earlier, in the *Real Lives* case, it had been the Home Secretary who protested. Now it was the Foreign Secretary, Sir Geoffrey Howe, who asked the Independent Broadcasting Authority not to transmit the programme. His main claim against it was that it might prejudice the inquest to be held in Gibraltar. It was indeed true that the programme would be available to the television system on Gibraltar, and that reports of it would be receivable through Spanish television or through the news programme provided by Independent Television News to the satellite Super Channel. But many objections immediately presented themselves – not least the fact that no date had yet been set for the Gibraltar inquest, and therefore even under

British law, had it prevailed, there could be no question of legal impropriety in publishing claimed eye-witness accounts.

The IBA had in the normal course of its regulatory function known about the programme, seen it, and in this case already taken its own legal advice – for by the time the matter came to the notice of the Foreign Office the programme was already being publicised in the normal manner. The chairman of the IBA, Lord Thomson, issued a prompt declaration that the programme would be transmitted, which it was. Nevertheless, within a matter of days it transpired that a current affairs team from BBC Northern Ireland had also been investigating the Gibraltar shooting and was about to transmit eye-witness accounts in the province. Again, the Foreign Secretary protested. Again, the broadcasting authority – this time, the Director General of the BBC in consultation with the Chairman of the Governors – rejected the argument. The programme went out to the Northern Ireland television audience but accompanied by detailed accounts of its content in national newspapers, and of course reported by international news organisations.

And in amongst the crises came the dramas. Alongside the procession of cases which centred on disputes between government and broadcasters over matters of fact – or at least of 'factual programmes' – was a series of controversies surrounding the work of the drama departments. Not that these involved government ministers directly, and certainly no Special Branch squad entered the fray. Nevertheless, the brouhaha in each case was of a highly-charged political nature, to which politicians were eager to contribute, and which critics in the press linked explicitly with other matters such as *Real Lives* when joining the attack on the BBC.

It may not have been mere accident that all of them, though very different, might, like most of the controversies already discussed, be said to have had defence issues at the heart of them, though one, a series called *The Monocled Mutineer*, was a period piece about a World War I soldier who deserted and was involved in a mutiny, uncovered in England years later. As drama it was widely admired, but not for the first time the BBC's own publicity machine sounded a confusing note, with a claim in an advertisement that this was 'a real life story', which, as crafted by the writer Alan Bleasdale, it was not. This was sufficient for the eternal problem of dramatising factual events ('drama-documentary', 'docu-drama', 'fiction' – choose your weapons) to be raised once more, but this time with charges that the piece was 'left-wing propaganda'. It might be noted that one newspaper editorial, in *The Times*, explicitly linked the drama series and the previous year's major political confrontation, when it wrote on the occasion of Duke Hussey's appointment as chairman of the BBC: 'He should examine the making and the marketing of *The Monocled Mutineer*'.

But the more sensitive issue, and the one in which some members of the government did take a closer interest, concerned the Falklands campaign. There were two projects, one written by Ian Curteis, author of previous well-received dramas on modern historical themes, including *Churchill And The Generals* and *Suez*, and the other by Charles Wood.

In a nutshell, the Curteis play was sparked by a conversation he had in October 1982, just a few months after the war, with the BBC's Director General, Alasdair Milne, at a lunch where Milne was speaking. Milne wondered about the war as a theme, and, some four years later, Ian Curteis was involved with the television drama department in pre-production work on his script, which he also sent to Milne. Two things happened: after various discussions internally, Peter Goodchild, head of television plays, went to see the writer with a view to making changes in the script; and Milne, learning during 1986 that it was scheduled for production in 1987 and screening around the fifth anniversary of the Falklands campaign in May, had it cancelled because it looked as though a general election would be called around that time (which it was) and the play would have to be shelved because of its depiction of figures involved in the election.

Milne says these were separate issues. Curteis sees them as coupled, claiming that among the reasons for cancellation was that television executives found its portrayal of Mrs Thatcher too sympathetic. The correspondence was voluminous; the play is now published for all to judge. In this context, the significance is the speed with which some in political circles seized upon the issue as a further weapon against the BBC. It was, we now know, one of the topics Mr Tebbit raised when he lunched at the BBC on 5 November, 1986 – the day, by chance, the corporation had published its response to his critique of the Libyan coverage. (He would not – ironically in the context of the *Secret Society* row that was yet to break – say anything about the work of the Cabinet Committee considering broadcasting policy.)

This was not, however, the end of the Falklands as an issue. Another writer, Charles Wood, and another BBC drama producer, were at work on a different piece, sparked by a newspaper report of an officer, gravely wounded in the assault on Mount Tumbledown, who felt he had been badly treated in the aftermath. This film, *Tumbledown*, was made, and screened in May 1988 to an advance chorus of protest, much of it to the effect that this was the 'left-wing' version of the Falklands whereas the BBC had suppressed the 'right-wing' version. In the event, it was clear that *Tumbledown* took no view of the rights and wrongs of the British action itself, a position for which it was indeed criticised by some writers, and that neither did politicians or their views figure in it. It focused, with great humanity, on the complex impact of war on the individuals caught up in it.

So why the row? The most perceptive analysis at the time seemed to me to come from Neal Ascherson, writing in the *Observer* a few days after the *Tumbledown* screening. The political establishment, as he saw it, saw 'our war' being hijacked by the media, as the Great War had been fixed with the image of lions led by donkeys, then Suez, then Vietnam. He went on:

> a bombardment fell on a humane and inoffensive programme which tried neither to mock nor to subvert. The main target was not *Tumbledown* but future Falklands War programmes to which it opened the way. But it was also true that *Tumbledown* had been marked down for attack, whatever its content turned out to be, by the partisans of Mr Ian Curteis. It will be recalled that Curteis wrote a 'Falklands play' for the BBC some years back, relating Mrs Thatcher to the conflict in a highly favourable way, and that production was cancelled when he and his director refused to accept changes in the script demanded from elsewhere in the BBC.
>
> So the Curteis work became 'our' Falklands drama, and the Richard Eyre production became 'theirs'. What interests me in this otherwise nonsensical polarity is the way in which a political group – the supporters of Mrs Thatcher – have appropriated a war.

Leaving aside the detail of who asked Ian Curteis to make what changes, and for what reason – matters which remain disputed and do seem to me the stuff of genuine controversy – Ascherson's view of the relationship between the two works as artificially created from the outside, for motives springing from political ideology, seem to be absolutely correct. We may, meanwhile, add to our catalogue of ironies: just as the attempts to suppress *Spycatcher* made Peter Wright's book a world best-seller, and him a millionaire, so the barrage of pre-publicity brought *Tumbledown* an audience approaching 11 millions, way above the normal expectation of a film of its kind in the midweek time-slot it occupied.

The third drama caught up in controversy came at much the same time as *Tumbledown*, and would be very much a footnote were it not for one particular element in it. The play was *Airbase*, a modest, expressionistic, rather wild, minority audience piece, whose small group of characters were the gung-ho, drugged-up crew of a British-based US bomber. It was serious about its message, but no more naturalistic in style than a war comic. Nevertheless, Conservative MPs rose against it, in one case claiming it as a slur on the USAF men based in his own constituency.

Equally appalled, in advance of seeing it, was a columnist in the *Independent* newspaper, William Rees-Mogg, former editor of *The Times*, who used the occasion – or rather, who wrote just ahead of the transmission of the play, which he apparently had not seen – to denounce the long-term decline in the BBC's standards in drama and journalism, which he dated back some 20 years to the era of Sir Hugh Greene's Director Generalship.

Rees-Mogg himself had been a governor, and for a time Deputy Chairman, of the BBC, through much of the period under consideration here, and played a critical role in the *Real Lives* affair. What may yet prove to be more significant, however, is his appointment by the Home Secretary, shortly after this column was written, as chairman of the proposed Broadcasting Standards Council. The significance will depend on the role the BSC itself comes to play, but for now one can reasonably see it as yet another intervention by government into broadcasting matters, and one that might almost have been calculated to apply more pressure, for there had been no discussion of its role, whether with the industry or in Parliament, and it is being established ahead of legislation, with few indicators of its intended role or scope. The result of a Conservative election manifesto pledge, a bolt from the blue in more senses than one, it seems to have a symbolic value, as an Awful Warning of what might come.

By this time, of course, one other major convulsion had taken place. The BBC itself was under new management. On Thursday, 29 January 1987, as the row over *Secret Society* reached a new pitch in the wake of the Special Branch's intervention with warrants from government law officers, Alasdair Milne became the first Director General of the BBC ever to be summarily dismissed from his office. In the lunch-break of a regular board of governors meeting at the BBC Television Centre, Marmaduke Hussey, who had taken up the appointment as Chairman a bare three months earlier, told him, as a unanimous decision of the board: 'We want you to leave immediately'.

Something of the sort had long been in the wind. By Alasdair Milne's own account, his relationship with the previous chairman, Stuart Young, who had died in the summer of 1986, and with the Deputy Chairman who spanned the Young and Hussey regimes, had often been tense, and Hussey evidently came in with a sense that the management of the BBC was in disrepair, a sense reinforced by most of his board. The conservative mid-set of new governors appointed by the Government throughout this period had already attracted public comment. Hussey's own Conservative connections were clear.

Milne, a man much admired by many who had worked with him, but no-one's idea of a diplomat, seems genuinely not to have sensed the trouble he was in within the corporation, as the headlines made by the BBC in cases like the ones cited here, and others, stacked up. The rights and wrongs of particular cases diminished in importance for governors who, one might hazard, had been appointed as public figures and did not enjoy taking flak of this sort.

Having in this period, therefore, neither the glory nor the power, they were perhaps vulnerable to the voices which reminded them of their title: were they or were they not Governors? Had a different analogy been chosen for the role, half a century ago, the perception of the relationship might have been different. Do the mere 'Members' of the Independent Broadcasting Authority possibly take a different view of their role?

The confusion and the unease certainly played a crucial role in the *Real Lives* débâcle, which arguably might have been contained – to the benefit of both broadcasters and government – had the Governors stuck to precedent and the advice of the Board of Management, and declined to preview the programme. In previewing it they actually raised the ante for the Home Secretary, Leon Brittan, whose unwise indication that he would use his powers to prevent the broadcast if they did not gave the whole affair the dimension of a constitutional crisis.

What it actually looked like was panic, by people who were either unaware of, or had forgotten, or chose to ignore (this last certainly applies to some governors) the reasons for certain conventions aimed at ensuring separation of powers. This applies to Mr Brittan, too, and cost him the job.

And the pressures behind the panic point to two other factors in the *Real Lives* affair which may be found elsewhere: Mrs Thatcher;

and the press. The genesis of what was in essence a three day event had the simplicity of a movie scenario: *Radio Times* published a feature about the impending programme; a *Sunday Times* reporter lobbed generalised questions about giving airtime to terrorists at the Prime Minister on tour in the USA; the *Sunday Times* plastered it across the top of its front page. The Home Secretary and the board of governors all got the message.

The role of the press is constantly significant and regularly malign in the relationship between politics and broadcasting. *Real Lives*, *Tumbledown*, the Tebbit attacks – would not have generated such heat had not newspapers gladly joined in. There are mixed motives in these things. Traditionally, television is seen as a rival to the press. Increasingly, newspaper owners have an interest in levering the broadcasting systems apart. As the individual reporters, leader writers, and headline writers weigh in, some of the results rest on sincerely held beliefs, others on the sense of a 'good story', some is straightforward 'bovver-boot' stuff. Whichever, the target is an easy one, and the outcome is liable to be a narrowing of positions.

The brutality of Milne's dismissal points to a shift in perception of the role of management and governors which seems to me to accord with wider changes of the Thatcher era, this narrowing of ideas included. (One of the more remarkable revelations in Alasdair Milne's book is of Norman Tebbit twice demanding a public correction of a statement by Milne's deputy, Alan Protheroe, to the effect that the BBC was against apartheid: so, Mr Tebbit said, was he, but the BBC was supposed to have no editorial opinion.)

There is a sense of relish, evident behind that William Rees-Mogg column and in other parts of the press, at turning a tide in ways of thinking and wiping out the writing in the sand – right back, in the case of the BBC, to the days of the overweening Sir Hugh Greene. It is a sense of old ideological scores being settled.

It has to be recognised that some of the scores might be real. Some paranoiacs do have real enemies. Liberals – and I use the word here to cover people in all political parties and none, at different times – have never demonstrated a total devotion to freedom of thought. There always have been fashions in what was deemed 'acceptable', or even 'interesting'. Even if the notion of seeking out 'right-wing playwrights' seems odd, given the essential conservatism of the vast majority of media output, a case like that of the unproduced Ian Curteis play poses questions supporters of *glasnost* should not wish to duck.

Nevertheless, looking back over the packed catalogue of events in the past three years, we can see how two apparently distinct strands – they might be labelled Secrecy and Suppression – knit together. The first is viewed as a technical matter (*Zircon*, Gibraltar, even perhaps denying the IRA 'the oxygen of publicity'), the second perhaps characterises Norman Tebbit's attempts to limit news coverage or the rows over *Tumbledown* and *The Monocled Mutineer*.

The British view of official secrets is now becoming an issue that crosses party divides (while uniting, on historical evidence, governments of whatever party). It is beyond the scope of this essay, yet it is worth noting that, in the case of the *Zircon* film, when Alan Protheroe, having sought various 'briefings', reported back to the BBC management that he now believed matters of security were involved and the film should not be shown, not everyone present agreed with him.

But official secret or otherwise, it all comes together in the end to form an ethos in which ideas that challenge, or could make life uncomfortable or risky, do not get taken up. One notices that new media entrepreneurs do not include challenge, or risk, on the programme side of the prospectuses, just the technological.

It has to be said, even so, that the outcome of all this activity has not been what the unknowing reader might have thought.

The *Real Lives* film, *The Edge of The Union*, was shown, two months late, with very minor changes which probably improved it.

Mr Tebbit's complaint over Libya was rejected and the then head of BBC television news has recently been promoted.

The two Gibraltar programmes were transmitted on schedule.

The Monocled Mutineer won prizes; *Tumbledown* pulled a huge audience and plaudits.

The radio series, *My Country Right Or Wrong*, was broadcast.

Of the two *Secret Society* documentaries, the *Zircon* film was eventually screened in September 1988, as part of a 'major' broadcast which appears to mean the input of other material. Again, an irony: only the film on Cabinet Committees will not be seen because, it is said, so much detail on the subject emerged in the press through the oxygen of publicity following the suppression that the film would now have to be extensively updated.

So all's well with the world? I conclude with two quotes.

Alasdair Milne again: 'By the Wednesday, Treasury solicitors were busy taking injunctions out against Campbell. The Select Committee on Defence were insisting on seeing the film but the Permanent

Secretary at the MOD, Sir Clive Whitmore, appeared to have refused them. On a couple of occasions, Hussey grumbled to me about why we ever came to make the film . . .'

And someone rather different. Richard Ingrams, former editor of *Private Eye*, now *Observer* columnist, had read in *The Times* that Mr Hussey, following a letter to that paper by the mother of a young woman portrayed in *Tumbledown*, was ordering a 'crack down' on television drama based on fact. The young woman, said Ingrams, had been shown the script in advance and had not objected:

> The thought that the BBC chairman might be swayed into banning an entire art-form by a letter in *The Times* from someone like Mrs Calder-Smith is not exactly reassuring . . . I should imagine that, once again, the BBC are less than pleased about the way in which their chairman blunders into controversy on the slightest pretext.

The same, on the other hand, might be said of some famous names on the political side of the fence.

3 Broadcasting: Silting up the Channels

Steven Barnett

On 14 November 1987 the UK's biggest selling newspaper, the *News of the World*, passed judgement on the BBC's adaptation of Olivia Manning's novels *Fortunes of War*. It was, they said, 'an expensive BBC drama disaster'. The basis for this sophisticated analysis of artistic merit was a comparison of the ratings: ITV had registered nearly 12 million viewers for *The Charmer* while on the other side *Fortunes of War* could muster no more than a 'paltry' 6.5 million. The five million readers of the *News of the World* could be forgiven for interpreting that as an informed and justifiable assessment of the corporation's output. And forgiven, too, for thinking that a great deal of their licence money had been squandered on a programme of little artistic merit and little popular appeal.

The story illustrates two of the least welcome consequences of a proliferation of TV channels. First, smaller audiences for all programmes will increase the pressure to produce programmes with the highest possible ratings. Second, those with controlling interests in both newspapers and television will seek to denigrate the programmes of rival channels in their newspaper columns. The *News of the World*, of course, is part of Rupert Murdoch's News International group; Murdoch also owns the satellite-delivered Sky Channel. This was neither the first nor the last example of a News International newspaper indulging in trenchant criticism of commercial broadcasting's most powerful rival – the BBC.

There will undoubtedly be a proliferation of new channels, and we should welcome the opportunities which television can provide for greater choice of viewing and greater freedom of expression. To reflect and encourage diversity – whether in cultural creativity, moral values or political beliefs – is a vital component of a healthy democracy.

We should remember, however, that viewers do not watch television channels, they watch television programmes. The conundrum for this Government (as for others in the Western world) is how to ensure that the new channels do indeed produce programmes which contribute to the diversity, creativity and freedom of speech which we in the UK have come to associate with our television and radio programmes over the last 60 years. Given our attachment to diversity and freedom of expression, what are the most effective constitutional and structural means of achieving these objectives?

This Government has made its position abundantly clear. In almost every field of human endeavour it embraces competition and the free market as the cornerstone of freedom and choice. This ideological commitment is applied to discussions of broadcasting policy with little understanding of the cultural consequences. The language of the free market has permeated the Peacock Report on Financing the BBC and the Green Paper on the future of radio. It is this Government's fervent belief that deregulation is the key to freedom and consumer choice.

Such notions have been challenged elsewhere. Other countries have recognised the implicit dangers of a deregulatory policy, and have accepted the need for a positive regulatory structure as the only means of achieving more open, enriching, diverse and enjoyable television and radio for *all* citizens. It is through a proper examination of other broadcasting systems, as well as through an understanding of what viewers and listeners want, that we can understand the consequences of a deregulatory policy for freedom of expression and cultural diversity.

It has become somewhat unfashionable to talk of 'public service broadcasting'. In a society increasingly driven by an individualist free enterprise culture, the phrase is perhaps too reminiscent of Reithian paternalism to strike a sympathetic contemporary chord. There are, however, certain elements of the public service tradition which are essential in any broadcasting system which aspires to openness and diversity and cultural enrichment. In particular:

1. Range. There should be a diversity of programmes from the relaxing to the demanding. As well as soap operas, quiz shows, feature films and news bulletins, audiences should have access to original drama, experimental comedy, arts programmes, science programmes, investigative documentaries and concerts. *The South Bank Show* and *Fortunes of War* are as vital to a healthy schedule as *Coronation Street* and *The Price is Right*.

2. Quality. Production values should be maintained, whether in the creation of a new soap opera, serialisation of a classic novel, or the production of a half-hour news programme. Both *News at Ten* and *I, Claudius* have won awards because they reached the highest standards within their genre.

3. Innovation. Programme makers should sometimes seek to lead, rather than follow, audience tastes. Experimentation should be encouraged, extending the boundaries of popular taste. Arguably, a generation of new, original comedy was pioneered by *Monty Python's Flying Circus*, which required courage and commitment from broadcasters. *The Singing Detective* was original drama which achieved almost unanimous critical acclaim, but bears no comparison with mainstream television serials.

4. Minority programming. Programmes should be available for a range of minority groups and interests, whether cultural minorities (Asians, Jews etc.), demographic minorities (the elderly, teenagers) or taste and interest minorities (jazz devotees, railway enthusiasts). Such programmes should not be relegated to the margin of schedules, but be easily accessible.

5. Distance from vested interests. Programmes should be subject neither to political nor commercial pressure. Editorial control should rest entirely with programme makers acting according to a non-partisan, professional code of conduct. *Panorama* and *World in Action* should be fearless in tackling awkward political questions, just as *That's Life* and *The City Programme* should be uncompromising in exposing fraudulent or unsavoury commercial practices.

6. Cultural identification. Programmes should reflect and enhance this country's cultural richness and diversity. A soap opera set in Manchester, Liverpool or East London; a Royal Wedding; an FA Cup Final or Test Match; a Shakespearean drama; or a series portraying the professional problems encountered by Heathrow customs officers all represent events, characters, and places of national interest. Any one of these programmes is substantially more expensive to produce than the equivalent length programme imported from the United States.

These requirements are embodied in the BBC's Charter and constitute part of the BBC's public service philosophy. To whatever extent it has succeeded or failed in these commitments, the aspirations of the BBC and its staff are manifest.

The private sector, on the other hand, would normally operate according to different dictates. For the legitimate objective of any private enterprise is to return a healthy profit. Television stations can provide that in abundance – if unchecked – by breaking every one of the principles outlined above; by scheduling nothing but cheap imported programmes to attract mass audiences at peak viewing times;

by avoiding the commercially contentious and the experimental; by paring budgets to produce programmes of the minimum quality acceptable a comparatively small outlay could return a very healthy profit. The consequence would be a homogeneous diet of ineffectual programmes which impoverish national culture, stifle national creative ability and fail to challenge the prevailing political orthodoxy.

A genuinely open and diverse broadcasting system therefore requires a legislative and regulatory framework to be applied to both public *and* commercial broadcasting. In the UK, the regulations applied to commercial television through the Independent Broadcasting Authority have been every bit as prescriptive as the BBC Charter. In return for their regional monopolies on advertising airtime, ITV companies must limit imported programmes to four hours of peak-time television per week; subscribe to ITN and transmit its Ten O'Clock News; limit advertising to seven minutes per hour overall; and plough back a reasonable proportion of their profits into original drama and factual documentaries. Renewal of their franchises depends ultimately on a proper fulfilment of these obligations.

Channel 4, meanwhile, operates according to a very specific statutory brief. It is wholly owned by the IBA who are charged with a duty to ensure that 'programmes contain a suitable proportion of matter calculated to appeal to tastes and interests not generally catered for by ITV'; and to 'encourage innovation and experiment in the form and content of programmes'.[1] Instead of competing for advertising revenue with ITV companies, it is financed through a levy on ITV revenue; in return, ITV companies are entitled to sell its advertising airtime.

Channel 4 represents the quintessence of regulation applied to the commercial sector in pursuit of cultural objectives deemed to be in the total national interest. Insulated from the market, and therefore liberated from the strait-jacket of mass audience programming, the new channel was given the structural support through which it could fulfil its statutory responsibility – to develop 'a distinctive character of its own'. Channel 4 is the child of the 1981 Broadcasting Act – a statute enacted under the present Conservative government.

Legislative arrangements have therefore ensured that commercial revenue has been harnessed to creative activity. As a direct result, many ITV companies are as concerned as the BBC to produce diverse, provocative and stimulating programmes. A free market approach to broadcasting will necessitate, by definition, the removal of these complex structural arrangements. We need not speculate on the consequences of such unrestrained competition since the free market experiences of other countries provide salutary lessons.

In 1985, the Government established the Peacock Committee to look into the future funding of the BBC. This spawned a plethora of economic, social and cultural comparative studies to assist the essentially economics-oriented committee in understanding the cultural consequences of any fundamental shift in funding. One of these studies, undertaken by the Centre for Television Research at Leeds University, was an international comparative review of the range and quality of output.[2] It examined three random mid-week days of programming between 6.00 and 11.00 pm in seven countries (table 3.1).

Table 3.1 Percentage time devoted to each category of programme content over three days, October 1985

	UK		France	Germany	Italy		Sweden	Australia		United States			
	BBC1	ITV	TF1	ZDF	RAI	Can5	TV1	TEN	ABC	ABC	CBS	NBC	PBS
1	28	20	13	15	16	–	15	16	14	23	24	23	29
2	10	9	–	10	6	–	8	–	21	–	–	–	13
3	17	14	27	8	12	41	3	10	2	7	8	8	–
4	27	30	7	21	11	16	12	12	16	49	33	46	–
5	7	–	15	11	19	11	27	21	5	–	15	–	–
6	–	–	–	–	4	–	24	–	5	–	–	–	29
7	5	9	16	15	4	3	7	–	16	–	–	–	23
8	5	3	–	5	3	–	2	17	11	–	–	–	–
9	–	13	7	7	11	27	–	20	–	17	18	20	–
10	1	2	15	8	13	3	2	3	11	3	2	3	6

Categories: 1=News; 2=Current Affairs; 3=Light Entertainment; 4=Series; 5=Plays/ Films; 6=Arts/religion/education; 7=Documentaries; 8=Sport; 9=Advertisements; 10=Other (incl. children, music, continuity).

Two observations stand out. First is the virtual disappearance of more serious programming from those commercial networks not subject to regulation. Current affairs are absent entirely from Italy's Canale 5, Australia's Channel Ten and every one of the American commercial networks. So are documentaries. For these three days, the American free market produced a schedule almost entirely dependent on a diet of news, adventure series and advertisements. The contrast with European public service channels is stark.

More illuminating is the UK example of how regulation can infuse a commercial operation. The ITV companies emerge with a remarkably similar diversity of programmes to the BBC, despite deriving all their revenue from advertising. The number of awards and the popularity of its exports also testify to the intrinsic quality of ITV programmes: *Jewel in the Crown*, *World in Action* and *Auf Wiedersehen Pet* are all monuments to the commercial sector's ability to match the BBC's international reputation.

The contrast with both the US and Australia is sharp. While in the US there are no conditions imposed on the three networks, and every programme stands or falls by the ratings, in Australia a legally constituted tribunal is required to maintain some control over the commercial networks. In practice, however, these networks command sufficient economic and political power to enable them to dictate their own terms. In both the US and Australia, as the table demonstrates, the national broadcasting organisations are reduced to filling the non-profitable gaps left by the hungry commercial networks. It is ironic that even these organisations – both the ABC and PBS – rely a good deal for their quality programmes on imports from the UK.

A second report demonstrates the consequences of the American free market in broadcasting. Through detailed interviews with senior network executives, this study examines the effects of a deregulated environment on network programming.[3]

There is implicit acknowledgement by network programmers that, through a subtle and almost insidious process, creativity, innovation and experimentation have been squeezed out by the increasingly voracious appetites of advertising agencies and marketing executives. Commercial imperatives are essentially conservative: advertisers demand the safety of last year's successes rather than the uncertainty of an untried playwright in an experimental drama. One American executive in this study was explicit:

> We don't want the young comer, the untried. We want the bankers. There's too much at stake. That's the attitude and we can't afford to do anything else.

Such a blunt appraisal of the innate conservatism within the American system should be compared both with the statutory duty of Channel 4 to innovate, and the encouragement within the BBC to develop originality. As one historian of British television comedy has written about *Monty Python's Flying Circus*: 'Part of the reason for the success of the series was that the BBC, having commissioned 13 programmes, left the team alone to get on with it'.[4] In short, American television lacks that crucial ingredient which can provide the inspiration for new, creative and culturally enriching programmes – the ability to take risks.

The potentially stultifying effects of a broadcasting system subjected to the free market are not confined to the elimination of innovation. According to one programme maker in the American study, they also dominate the creative process of drama production.

> The amount and timing of advertising have formative implications for programme content ... climaxes and artificial cliff-hangers must be regularly built into the dramatic structure of series episodes, so that viewers will be motivated to stay tuned once the commercial break is over.

Most crucially of all, the free market has implications for current affairs coverage. It is often said of commercial broadcasters that they are at least beyond the reach of politicians. There are, therefore, no temptations to bend with the prevailing political winds in order to secure adequate funding. If some publicly funded broadcasters find themselves at odds with their political masters through their news and current affairs output (and the BBC's problems are by no means unique), American networks are in many ways even more beholden to their commercial masters.

During the 1984 presidential election, for example, no attempt was made to lengthen news bulletins which remained constant at 22 minutes. Campaign news, according to the Leeds study, was geared to the spectator of a political horse race 'rather than to the needs of a prospective information seeker or to a citizen wanting to make up his mind how to vote'. More generally, the system militates against searching, challenging, or hard-hitting investigative current affairs and documentary programmes: 'The networks, in order to survive in a free market economy, must make sure that they do not have too many controversial or difficult programmes in their schedules because they run the risk of losing a fair amount of money on each of them'.

It was repeatedly claimed, when ITV's *This Week* televised its controversial investigation into the SAS shooting of alleged IRA terrorists in Gibraltar, that the BBC could not have withstood the immense political pressure exerted on the IBA to withdraw the programme. The IBA stood firm, and an important, challenging and professional piece of investigative journalism was broadcast. But there is a very real threat that in a deregulated television environment political pressure will be rendered superfluous. One of the foundations of a democratic society – the legitimate power of broadcasters to ask difficult and embarrassing questions of political leaders – will be emasculated by an increasing dependence on advertisers and their attendant demands for predictability and safety.

There is little value in a structure which fails to fulfil audience demands. Accusations of paternalism could, with some justification, be levelled at those who seek to impose a structure of broadcasting without due regard for the tastes and interests of viewers. Indeed, the legitimacy of the free market solution is derived, say its proponents, from the ability of the market to adapt itself to the wishes of consumers. This analysis suggests that aggressively competitive commercial channels concentrate on a narrow range of programmes precisely because viewers, by inclination, prefer a fairly narrow diet of programme types.

Analysis of UK audience data, however, proves conclusively that viewers take full advantage of the range of programmes available.[5] Table 3.2 shows how one week's viewing in March 1985 broken down into programme categories:

Table 3.2   Proportion of total viewing for different programme types March 1985

	Entertainment				Demanding		
Light Ent	Light Drama	Films	Sport	Drama/ Arts	Info	News	Children & misc.
17	21	8	9	7	20	11	5

Despite the availability of substantially more entertainment programming, viewers generally devote no more than 55 per cent of viewing time to such programmes compared to 43 per cent 'more demanding' programmes. The authors demonstrate, moreover, that the appetite for a wide range of programmes is consistent across all sectors of the population and does not vary according to age, social class, geographical location or any other demographic variable. *Panorama* is watched by all classes and age groups, and is not the exclusive preserve of the more educated; *Dallas* appeals to a complete cross section of the population.

Minority programmes, too, are watched by nearly all viewers: '40 out of 50 million people choose to watch several low rating programmes on BBC2 each week, for an average of some two hours each. And well over 30 million dip into Channel 4 for an hour or more'. Again, this is true for all sectors of the population: even the lowest rated minority programme will generally be watched by a complete cross section of viewers.

This report concludes that the current mix of light and serious programming does not prejudice the tastes of one sector of the population in favour of another; consequently, any major shift in the existing balance would be to the detriment of *all* viewers. Any structural change which enlarges the repertoire of one category of programmes but ultimately diminishes another would be a disservice to *all* viewers.

Viewers and listeners also demonstrate by their own opinions a commitment to diversity and innovation. In public attitude surveys undertaken by the Broadcasting Research Unit,[6] for example, two-thirds of viewers were committed to the proposition that television producers should experiment even if programmes turn out not to be worth watching. A similar proportion approved of Channel 4's policy of commissioning programmes for minority groups, whether or not they themselves watch them. A huge majority – over 90 per cent – believed that television has a duty to inform people about news and current affairs. Over two-thirds support the continued existence of Radio 3 despite its tiny two per cent share of total radio listening.

The sixty year old traditions of British broadcasting are not founded on public hostility or even indifference, but on thorough public endorsement. An audience which demonstrates by its behaviour an appreciation of a range of programmes and by its attitudes an acceptance of experimentation, minority programming and adequate news and information services, will not be served by a structure which offers a greater number of television programmes within a diminishing spectrum of variety.

By exploiting satellite transmission technology (and a new generation of receiving dishes costing no more than £200) it will soon be possible for most UK households to receive several additional channels by direct broadcast. It is estimated that the number of hours of European television will have increased from 186 000 to 475 000 by the end of 1990; this expansion will be predicated entirely on commercial funding.

These direct broadcast channels can be divided into two categories. Firstly, those directed specifically at one country, and therefore within that country's jurisdiction: British Satellite Broadcasting, due to provide three extra channels by the end of 1989, is to be regulated by the IBA and falls into this category. Secondly, those trans-frontier enterprises which cover a wide area of Europe and attempt to schedule an eclectic mixture of programmes aimed at a European audience. This group includes Murdoch's Sky Channel, and the more recently launched Super Channel.

The trans-frontier satellite channels pose difficult problems of sovereignty and control. They are bound by no regulations. They are accountable to no authority, statutory body or elected group of overseers, and it is doubtful whether Messrs Murdoch, Maxwell and Berlusconi have invested huge capital sums in transnational broadcasting primarily out of concern for Europe's cultural welfare.

Additional entertainment-based channels can, of course, make a positive contribution to the total available television. They do, however, pose a threat to individual countries which is concentrating the collective European mind. Almost to a state, the countries of Europe are examining their structures, planning the introduction of television advertising where it was previously forbidden, hastening plans for an extra channel, and relaxing rules on prescribed times or products for advertising – overriding their own national inclinations in opposition to the new satellite channels.

There are also less obvious programming effects. The pan-European channels are provoking defensive and retaliatory actions from the traditional broadcasters, concerned to retain both audiences and advertising revenue for the domestic economy. The Leeds study quoted above provides several examples of a growing tendency for European broadcasters to seek out the mass audience. Thus, in Germany, 'marketing criteria are increasingly determining the broadcasters' decisions on programme structure and content'; RAI schedules in Italy reveal a growing preponderance of entertainment programming; Dutch broadcasting has become more 'commercial in spirit if not in structure and finance' with more light entertainment, quizzes, chat shows and game shows. In France, television has moved 'closer to matching, without totally imitating, the recipes for success and programming schedules of American and European commercial television networks'.

No such movements have been made in the UK because satellite channels have only been available to the tiny proportion of cable homes; there has therefore been no threat to ITV advertising revenue. 1989 will herald the arrival not only of the new UK-directed BSB, but the beaming of Rupert Murdoch's Sky Channel direct to any household with the requisite receiving equipment. We have, arguably, already witnessed the first shots in a consolidation campaign by ITV: on 12 June 1988 its flagship current affairs programme

Weekend World was killed off, with no plans for a similar replacement. One commentator, at least, was in no doubt about the cause: 'The episode raises the question of whether ITV ... can be trusted to take current affairs seriously in the long term, as it expends its creative energies on plans to attract more viewers, appease advertisers, and draw up battle orders to compete with the satellite television antics of Rupert Murdoch and British Satellite Broadcasting'.[7] Once again, a programme with a reputation for thoughtful and challenging contributions to understanding current affairs and contemporary society is silenced by the commercial imperative.

In this case, however, the commercial imperative is more imagined than real. Independent companies will argue with the IBA that programming requirements must be relaxed in preparation for the imminent competition, but there is no evidence that this competition will be anything but marginal for some time to come.

This challenge to the conventional wisdom, that large numbers of British viewers will wish to take advantage of the new viewing opportunities, is based not on speculation but on empirical fact. By April 1988, additional channels – including Sky – were available via cable to around 1.4 million households in the UK. No more than 17 per cent elected to take advantage of this additional choice; and even those who have subscribed spend most of their viewing time watching the terrestrial channels. The erosion of factual or documentary programming in anticipation of a threat which may never materialise is a disturbing trend.

There is a second, far graver cause for concern at any reduction in news and information programmes on national channels. Rupert Murdoch has announced that, as well as bringing Sky to the British market via the direct broadcast Astra satellite, he has plans to use the same route for at least two more channels – one of which will be a news and film channel. Satellite delivered transnational channels are subject to none of the safeguards for balance and impartiality which govern all terrestrial channels in the UK. Those familiar with the standards of news reporting in Murdoch's News International newspapers – *The Times*, *Sunday Times*, *Sun*, *News of the World*, *Today* – may question the news channel's commitment to informed, objective and non-partisan reporting.

The UK, like most democratic countries, has fostered a tradition of editorial independence in all factual television programmes. It is a tradition based on the power of television imagery to influence political opinion, and is a condition of television reporting supported by an overwhelming proportion of the British population. Satellite-delivered channels which are beyond the jurisdiction of any single country are subject to no such obligations, and will be vulnerable to editorial influence. Even if there was no explicit attempt at influencing opinion through manipulation of news stories, news editors can be tempted into an insidious process of distortion simply be anticipating the editorial line most acceptable to their employer. The implications of unregulated news channels for unbiased and impartial reporting of factual events are particularly disturbing.

For all these reasons, it is imperative that those channels which have traditionally been bound by obligations based on the principles of free, open and diverse broadcasting stand firm in their programming priorities; and that those responsible for developing the legislative framework find some means of imposing international agreements on trans-frontier satellite channels. Whatever the role of new channels, evidence suggests that audiences will still depend on the terrestrial national broadcasters for the vast majority of viewing.

According to the Director of the International Institute of Communications, 'it seems inevitable that broadcasting policy will wither away in the next few years'.[8] He attributes this process of degeneration to a battle of government departments: the Home Office which 'sees Britain as a society, and therefore supports the idea of broadcasting as a public service' and the Department of Trade and Industry which 'sees Britain as an economy and encourages competition'.

The prevailing ideological view is undoubtedly predicted on the DTI perspective: a conviction that the market is the proper mechanism for determining what 'consumers' want. Broadcasting might, incidentally, produce television programmes but ultimately it is an industry which should be subject to the same disciplines as the furniture or baked beans industries. The lessons from other countries, the impoverished nature of broadcasting systems based on the free market, the express wishes of majorities of citizens which plainly cannot be fulfilled by the free market, go unheeded.

Unregulated competition as applied to the commercial world is inappropriate for broadcasting, and plainly results in a diet of television programmes inconsistent with what viewers want to see. Competition is no more than a battle for the largest audiences to suit advertisers. It diminishes the range of programmes on offer; stifles creative, imaginative and experimental drama; frustrates investigative journalism and documentaries on important contemporary issues; swamps any attempt to satisfy minorities with programmes directed at homogeneous majorities; militates against quality production in every area of programming except light entertainment; and could ultimately undermine an essential feature of every democracy, a guaranteed source of impartial and untrivialised news and information. Ultimately, it is the advertiser who sets the programming agenda rather than the viewer or programme maker.

It has been said that we will always have the BBC. Its reassuring presence, available to the whole population with its licence fee revenue safeguarded, should guarantee an independent voice in serious current affairs and news programming while commercial channels compete in the production of lighter material.

This notion is misconceived and dangerous for two reasons. First, both PBS in America and ABC in Australia demonstrate that a marginalised public broadcaster with little popular appeal, relegated to a diet of serious-minded programming, becomes increasingly impoverished and impotent. There is an almost inevitable spiral of lower audiences and lower funding resulting in generally inferior programming. A public broadcaster in this position cannot afford to take risks with unusual comedy, unknown playwrights or minority sports; nor can it afford to jeopardise relations with the government of the day. Even a public broadcaster with a charter and mandate must ultimately justify a universal fee by providing universal programmes: *EastEnders* is as vital a part of the BBC's remit as *Newsnight* and *The Singing Detective*.

The second problem is even more fundamental. As commercial channels proliferate, politicians in all countries will inevitably begin to question the need for public money – or a licence fee – to subsidise non-commercial channels. We were afforded a glimpse of the logic which might be expected to prevail in the 1990s by the Home Secretary in 1988:

> As choice multiplies and the average viewer has more and more channels to choose from, it will become less and less defensible that he should have to pay a compulsory licence fee to the BBC.[9]

So how, in a rapidly changing technological environment, should the BBC be funded? This too was explained: 'Subscription enables the viewer to pay precisely for what he wants and I am sure that this is a direction in which the BBC should move'.

It is a disturbing vision. By removing the BBC from the public domain, by making it available only to those prepared to pay a subscription fee inevitably larger than the licence, the government would be depriving a significant proportion of the population – unable or unwilling to pay – of the only non-commercial voice in broadcasting. It would also be forcing on it the very same commercial imperatives of less risk taking, fewer minority programmes and more homogeneous programming as the BBC seeks to maximise its subscription base.

It is a policy option which is explicitly rejected by the independent report commissioned by the Home Office on the viability of subscription channels. Its conclusion was unambiguous:

> Scrambling the BBC services *only* would neither be viable – that is, the channels would not raise enough revenue to cover costs – nor would it be in the public interest – that is, substantial losses in consumer welfare would result as a consequence of the exclusion of non-subscribers from the benefits of BBC television viewing.[10]

Finally, it is a policy which conflicts with Mr Hurd's own vision of the future for radio. Both the government's Green Paper on Radio, and the Home Secretary in successive speeches, have emphasised the vital and valuable role of the BBC in 'sustaining radio services of a range and quality admired throughout the world'.[11] There has not yet been an explanation of how BBC radio will be funded should its television services be required to operate on a subscription basis. Given the hostile environment for non-commercial broadcasting, it is not unthinkable that BBC radio – without any philosophical or financial commitment – will also be left to wither away.

It is ironic that the country which is internationally recognised as the producer of some of the world's best television and radio programmes, and which pioneered a public service system adopted in some form in most other countries, should now be surrendering its hard-won superiority to the 'free market' of new technology. Other countries, rather than adopt an unthinking ideological approach, have given exhaustive briefs to committees of enquiry to investigate the consequences of unfettered technological development. One conclusion from the Canadian Task Force was not untypical of other countries' concerns:

> To understand the implications of technology is one thing, to surrender to it another. The fact that culture is at stake cannot be overlooked.[12]

New Zealand, too, is concerned about the possibility of a decline in programme standards which might be accelerated by independence on a diet of mass entertainment. Its committee was unequivocal:

The Commission does not believe that the unfettered play of market forces in broadcasting would satisfy the range of public demands which were made clear to us throughout the submissions.[13]

The real danger of an unregulated free-for-all is an atmosphere of creative sterility and intellectual conformity which would impoverish rather than enrich British society. If any doubt should remain about the consequences, perhaps the last word should come from an official government report in the country which epitomises the free market model:

There is a sense in which Americans are denied what other societies consider vital: a flourishing public communications service uncensored by commercial imperatives.[14]

Genuine choice, genuine diversity and genuine freedom of speech requires the implementation and strict observance of properly thought out constraints on commercial broadcasting as well as an adequately funded and universally available non-commercial broadcaster. Just as naked political interest should not be allowed to determine the content of programmes in a genuine democracy, neither should naked commercial interest. Paradoxically, *glasnost* in British broadcasting depends ultimately on effective regulation.

Notes

1. *Broadcasting Act 1981*, Section 11(1).
2. *Programme Range and Quality – an International Comparison*. Centre for Television Research, Leeds University, June 1986.
3. *Television in the United States: Funding Sources and Programming Consequences*, Jay G. Blumler, Centre for Television Research, Leeds University, January 1986.
4. *From Fringe to Flying Circus*; Roger Wilmut, London, 1980.
5. *Advertisers or Viewers Paying?* A.S.C. Ehrenberg, London Business School, February 1986.
6. See, for example, *The Listener Speaks*, April 1988; *Keeping Faith?*, January 1988; *Invisible Citizens*, October 1986.
7. Maggie Brown in the *Independent*, 13 July 1988.
8. John Howkins in the *Listener*, 14 April 1988.
9. Speech to the Coningsby Club by Douglas Hurd, 22 June 1988.
10. *Subscription Television: a Study for the Home Office*; Booz Allen and Hamilton; HMSO, May 1987.

11. Address to the Radio Academy Festival by Douglas Hurd, 6 July 1988.
12. Report of the Task Force on Broadcasting Policy, Government of Canada, September 1986.
13. *Broadcasting and Related Telecommunications in New Zealand*; Report of the Royal Commission of Inquiry, September 1986.
14. *A Public Trust*: Report of the Carnegie Commission on the Future of Public Broadcasting, New York, 1979.

4 VAT, A Tax on Knowledge
The Earl of Stockton

The invention of printing put a powerful instrument into the hands of mankind. Too powerful, perhaps, for either church or state. Its introduction into England was therefore not surprisingly closely followed by action to weaken its new and liberating effects. Eventually, and ingeniously, the book trade itself was called in to deal with its own dangerously threatening consequences. In 1956 Mary Tudor and her husband Philip of Spain granted a Charter to the Worshipful Company of Stationers declaring that the King and Queen, 'wishing to provide a suitable remedy against the seditious and heretical books which were daily printed and published, give certain privileges to their beloved and faithful lieges, the 97 Stationers.'

The Charter's many provisions instituted what may well have been the first closed shop of many in the printing and publishing trade, for it laid down that no one in the realm should exercise the art of printing either himself, or through an agent, unless he were a freeman of the Stationers' Company of London, or unless he had royal permission to do so.

Authority was also vested in the Master and Warden of the Company, to search the houses and premises of all printers, bookbinders, and booksellers in the kingdom for any printed matter, to seize (and treat as they thought fit) anything printed contrary to any statute or proclamation, and to imprison anyone who printed without the proper qualification or resisted their search. Such offenders were to remain in gaol for three months without trial and be fined £5, half of which was to go to the Crown and half to the Company – an ingenious blend of incentive payments and national taxation!

This strange mixture of the totalitarian (with provisions reminiscent of those introduced in 1928 by Stalin) and the capitalist (privatisation of the fines to be extracted by the Company) was of course, principally to stamp out the religious freedom which had begun to emerge during the reign of Henry VIII. This beginning ushered in a continuous history of censorship of the written word, either by pre-censorship or by taxation in the form of Stamp Acts. From the earliest days of printing, therefore, control of information and of ideas became a major preoccupation and objective of government.

It was not until 1855 that the last Stamp Tax on the press was abolished by the then Chancellor of the Exchequer, Gladstone. It was expunged with a solemn declaration from Parliament that there should be no 'taxes on knowledge'. This principle has been honoured ever since, even during the meagre days of the Second World War when British taxation inevitably was at an all-time high. An attempt *was* made, however, in 1940, right at the height of the Battle of Britain, to bring in a tax on books. It was demolished by A.P. Herbert who demanded of the miserable Chancellor, Kingsley Wood: 'Did he want to limit the consumption of Bibles and Prayer Books? . . . he would go down in history as the first Chancellor of the Exchequer to put a tax on the word of God!'

Today the possibility of a tax on books is once more confronting us. And ironically, like 1940, the threat again comes from across the Channel. This time from the Common Market as it moves towards harmonisation of Value Added Tax.

Any discussion of a sales tax on books sooner or later runs up against the principle that such a tax should have no loophole. It is claimed that to make exceptions is to create unfair distortions because those products which pay tax subsidise those which do not. In practice, of course, the cold-blooded application of such principles creates more unfairness than it prevents.

There are today, as much as ever, one or two absolute fundamentals of existence which no income group should be asked to forego, and which should be made easy to obtain. All British governments have accepted this in the past, as does Mrs Thatcher today in her consistent pledge not to tax basic foodstuffs. She recognises that this would victimise the lowest income group, since the cost of basic foodstuffs absorbs such a large proportion of their income.

No one suggests that a tax on books is as obviously regressive as a tax on food. People are not physically threatened by their absence, just as they can survive without windows in their homes. But a book tax, like the infamous window taxes of the past, is more subtly regressive. In theory both may be neat solutions. In practice they victimise those people to whom a marginal increase in availability is the difference between blindness and sight. And both are examples of why a government should beware of pursuing some Holy Grail of fiscal symmetry. In fiscal matters pure theory should always bow to political and social reality.

In this questioning and perhaps philistine age we need once more to spell out in detail why books deserve a tax-free status in our civilisation.

The written word is second only to the spoken word as a form of communication. As a means of recording ideas, developing them and transferring them from generation to generation, written words – and books in particular – are supreme. The intellectual capacity of a single human today is probably no greater than it was in Cro-Magnon times. But collective intelligence of society today is infinitely greater, because through books we have been able to concentrate and direct the accumulated wisdom of our forbears. To flick through those pages of the *Bookseller* which list the week's British publications – sometimes 20 pages with 100 titles to the page – is to touch the pulse of our civilisation. Books remain the essential ingredient in a civilisation's growth. The politician has always recognised the importance of books and, according to the political mood, bans, burns or encourages them. Mary Tudor ordered the burning of books (just as she ordered the burning of those fathers of the Church of England who wrote them). Gladstone ordered the abolition of the Stamp Acts because he wanted to extend the franchise. He did not expect a newly enfranchised populace to vote responsibly if they were illiterate and uninformed. In the government's own archives there is a splendid film, made in 1941 by the Ministry of Information, capitalising on the fact that not even in wartime did Britain resort to a tax on books. (Though, as we have seen, they nearly did!) The film compares free, civilised Britons reading what they liked, with brutish, jack-booted Nazis burning books. Admittedly this is classic propaganda footage, but today's Chancellor cannot but be mindful of the fundamental political truth behind the vivid imagery: books are important.

Now we have a democratically elected government with a mandate from the British people to introduce change and reform on a wide scale. It has questioned vested interest and restrictive practice in many quarters. It is still questioning the protected place of books in the tax system, and the book trade has answered, as it did in 1940, 1957, 1969 and 1985, that books merit such protection in a civilised society. For, if the cause of books is considered a vested interest, it is an interest vested in our civilisation, our freedom and our future. And if that case could be proved in the darkest days of World War II at a time of even greater pressure on the British Government's borrowing requirement! – it can surely be proved today.

The battle continues to be waged to restore Britain's competitive position within the Community, and to raise the nation's living standards. It is estimated that the store of knowledge in the world today is nine times greater than the entire accumulation up to the Second World War. The pool is doubling in size every eight years. This knowledge explosion has huge implications for our civilisation.

At the present time the Government is investing £18 billion in formal education. By 1991 the figure will rise to £19.2 billion.[1] Books are bound inextricably with this investment. A statistical analysis[2] of the number of titles published in Britain between 1984 and 1986 from aeronautics to travel guide books, shows that over 80 per cent may be regarded as primarily educational or cultural. Within this listing, Medical Science and Psychology have increased by 71.4 per cent – 8 per cent of all titles; and Religion and Theology–Philosophy by 110 per cent – 5.6 per cent of all titles. In terms of the money value of these categories, again 80 per cent of the total can be classified as being of educational or cultural merit. This latter breakdown shows that one third of the market is devoted to specific school and university publications. Reference books, maps and religious works comprise 8.8 per cent. A further quarter of the market is occupied by adult non-fiction, biographies, hobby books and so on, with children's reading adding in another 10 per cent or so.

Ultimately, of course, a really definitive breakdown of which books are 'worthy' is impossible – even for the taxman! To draw distinction between the degree of benefit and the degree of entertainment in a single book, or between tomorrow's GCSE text and today's best-seller, is an impossible task. A Ladybird book in the hands of a cabinet minister may be only marginally educational, but it is advanced stuff for a three year old! It would indeed be a fruitless distraction to argue that the tax man can draw fiscal, any more than critical, distinctions between one title and another.

It is not difficult to predict the consequences of a general sales tax. To any low income family food is an absolute necessity for the continuation of life. Books, however important, command no such absolute; and the most vulnerable individuals will suffer. The under-privileged child who looks to the school to provide books; the teacher battling to help a functionally illiterate school leaver; the unemployed person who takes up study to retrain himself; the single woman with a family to rear; the handicapped and the bedridden – all these will be the first victims of a tax on reading.

Data published in 1984 in the *British Journal of Social Psychology* by Peter Warr of Sheffield University gives evidence from a wide sample of how people reallocate their time when they become unemployed. 48 per cent reported that they read more newspapers, 31 per cent that they read more books, and 13 per cent that they read more books for study. This compares with only two per cent who said they had started going to new classes or courses. No particular correlation was found between unemployed reading and age group, or between reading patterns and length of time unemployed, although generally those who read more have a stronger sense of well-being. The evidence shows that the unemployed turn to reading as a major pastime and that books provide the major source of self-help and retraining for the unemployed.

Very similar results, showing that unemployed people read more books than employed people earning salaries up to £9000 per annum, were revealed in a computer analysis of the Target Group Index 1984. Indeed 10.6 per cent of the unemployed buy ten or more books per year as compared with a national average of 9.5 per cent. Significantly, these results were corroborated by the high level of newspaper and magazine reading by the unemployed as shown in an analysis of the 1984 National Readership Survey. For a government which professes to believe in self-help and retraining and deplores the 'nanny state', a tax on the books of the unemployed would seem curiously inconsistent!

Students, necessarily, have one of the highest levels of book buying of all groups. According to government figures, given a 15 per cent book price increase, their grants would have to rise by £15 million if their level of buying were to be maintained. It would be £5 million more if the final price rise due to lost economies of scale were included. Students also borrow heavily from libraries. They would find this much harder were VAT to be imposed. Today university and other libraries in higher education buy 20 per cent fewer books than five years ago. These are catastrophic figures. Their need has massively increased in line with the information explosion. And, seriously compounding the problem, schools and public libraries have also been forced to cut back drastically on their spending because of the general cut in the local authority Rate Support Grant by the Government and their rate-capping of certain authorities.

If this two-pronged attack on student reading were not to be reimbursed then the tax would represent a thinly-disguised clawback of education spending, conceived to stifle perhaps the most cost-effective agent in university life – the book.

The Government estimates that VAT on books would raise

approximately £85m in gross revenue. But this assumes that the level of book sales would remain the same, whereas all the evidence indicates that sales would fall. The gross revenue would therefore be lower and, indeed, the final net yield to the Government could well be nothing at all.

When book prices rise faster than general prices, demand for books falls proportionately. In Britain between 1974 and 1984 this was proved true. From 1972 to 1980 book prices closely followed the pattern of price increases for other consumer products. The demand for books remained constant. During the next two years, due to rising paper and production costs, book prices outstripped the cost of living – a rise of 14.8 per cent as compared to about 10 per cent for other consumer prices. This was accompanied by a fall in book sales of 5.7 per cent in each of these two years. This experience is confirmed by studies conducted in the USA and Ireland. We can conclude from this that the large atypical rise in book prices following VAT would cause a similarly severe contraction in sales.

In publishing (whether books or newspapers) an unusually large proportion of the costs are in overheads. This means that when demand falls economies of scale are reduced, and the unit price increases. The chain reaction of rising price and falling demand continues.

A 15 per cent VAT rate would cause a 19 per cent drop in the book market. This reduces the Government's estimated £85m tax yield to £70m. But in addition there would be a £10m drop in corporation tax; a £40m increase in the unemployment bill (8000 jobs – 3000 from publishing and 5000 from bookshops); a £10m drop in income tax and at least an additional £1m in tax collection costs! In fact the Government would be only £9m better off in real terms. And if they compensated students and libraries for their loss the Government would be losing money in real terms. If the Government were then to introduce subsidies to authors (as happens elsewhere in Europe even where VAT is charged at a nominal rate) its profit and loss account would slip further into the red.

Further, tax relief on books would avoid the charge of government censorship, whether accidental or deliberate, which the direction of subsidy to certain income groups or certain authors would bring. Incidentally, tax relief on books is a very inexpensive way of helping to provide an important element of education and even democracy to the broad mass of the population.

Why then has VAT on books been mooted at all? Perhaps it is

partly because the true net yield of the tax has not been sufficiently calculated. Partly it may be the short memory of politicians – or the complexity of the argument.

And why has the question been re-opened now? It is suggested that with the introduction of the 'internal market' in 1992, the EEC will force Britain to tax books like other commodities if we do not go ahead and do it voluntarily.

Several points should be borne in mind, however, when this argument is made. First, there is no such thing as pan-European tax harmony. For example, some EEC countries tax motorway travel; but there is no suggestion that we must therefore put up motorway toll booths in Britain. Secondly, even among those EEC countries which do tax the written word, *all*, without exception, apply a reduced rate to at least one form of publishing. Thirdly, these reduced rates differ from country to country – and in the case of Italy is as low as two per cent.

In addition, those countries which do tax books invariably plough back more than they receive, in the form of grants to authors and subsidies (overt and covert) to their publishing companies. Such subsidies are inevitably inefficient and open to abuse, and have never been requested by the British publishing industry.

From the most recent meeting in Brussels on the question of VAT harmonisation (April 1988) the view emerging is that the original plan for a 'Europe without frontiers' by Lord Cockfield, the Commissioner for the Internal Market, must be modified to meet UK concerns. Talk is now of 'approximation' rather than 'harmonisation' with VAT rates falling into two broad bands, one between 14 and 20 per cent and another between four and nine per cent for basic items. But even this is regarded by London government and financial circles as unnecessary and not acceptable. Our present Chancellor's view, made at the Anglo-German Konigswinter Conference in Cambridge, is that the Cockfield VAT plan was a 'bureaucratic *non sequitur*' from the start. The EEC's 1992 programme, in Mr Lawson's judgement, should be focused on deregulation rather than harmonisation.[3]

So the EEC itself is already split on this issue in many ways and at many levels. If books retain tax exemption in the UK, EEC policy itself might eventually be changed. However, if we surrender this feature of our tax system, we will certainly not be able to retrieve it. Not only will the guiding precedent have been removed, but the dead hand of Brussels (while willing to ignore an uncontroversial failure to pursue what is at best a very nebulous 'harmony') would surely be raised against the act of open deharmonisation such as some future abolition of the tax on books would involve.

Nevertheless, it is clear that 1992 will not arrive without the question of VAT on books being seriously addressed yet again by the British Government. Perhaps the most realistic political assessment of an achievable compromise *is* the adoption of a community-wide basis of a multiple rate system with perhaps as many as three separate rates. These would be a necessities rate of 0–5 per cent, a standard rate of 15 per cent, and a luxury rate of from 25–40 per cent. This would allow the British Government both to retain the first rate for commodities to which it is committed (and to which should be added publications!), while at the same time keeping in tune with European harmonisation.

There are, however, a number of very grave problems in the way of achieving this objective. Lord Cockfield's argument that VAT differentials will distort trade in a frontier-free market has met with scepticism in Whitehall and yet the British Government seems unlikely to be prepared to fight this battle, for it would be bound to delay the full implementation of harmonisation of the market by the prescribed date. France has drawn up its own report on the likely cost to the French economy. (They also have a rooted Cartesian objection to zero being regarded as a number, and claim that this is illogical since it is, by definition, without value!) Spain and Portugal would have to increase indirect taxation, while the Danes and Italians would have to implement cuts.

There are numerous internal reasons why the book business is concerned about any tax on the written word. Such reasons have entered this argument only as bald additions to the Government's unemployment benefit bill, and dark hints about the reduced variety and availability of books. That is as it should be, since in most cases, 'ad misericordiam' pleading is of little interest to politicians or the general public. Rather, what has been seen here is evidence that a tax on books is a regressive, even barbaric step; that for little or no yield, to satisfy a curious desire for uniformity in our inevitably disordered worlds, or in response to some foreign pressure which does not in reality exist, a tax might be imposed in the next budget which would turn back 128 years one not inconsiderable part of the democratic progress of this country.

Although the disadvantaged and the student would be the first to suffer, the final whirlwind would not be reaped for several years, when the heirs of those who acceded to the tax inherited a country which had lost its technical and competitive qualifications, and a political system which was increasingly vulnerable to misinformation and manipulation.

There are those who say that the book trade is being unduly alarmist. Well, I am not an hysteric, but nor am I an ostrich. The threat of taxation on the printed word is not only unnecessary, uneconomic and essentially illiberal, but the mechanisms of its imposition are, I suspect, probably corrupt and tyrannical in the most insidious fashion.

I do not wish to ascribe ulterior or suspect motives to members of any political party in Britain, nor would I dare to impugn the actions or aspirations of any civil servant in Whitehall today, but if we allow this tax to be imposed on the publishing industry we shall be branded as appeasers of tyranny, and rightly so. For we shall have opened the way to control of publication by the state and the gradual but inevitable erosion of the freedoms of speech and expression that have been won with difficulty, pain and blood.

No government in this country, whether of the far right, the wet middle or the extreme left has yet introduced 'newspeak', and there is a certain Orwellian irony that the last time we successfully defended the printed word was in 1984.

Printed and spoken English is an asset of unimaginable value to this country. The story of the emergence of English as the most powerful, influential and significant language in the history of the world is well known, and yet successive British governments have refused, through lack of vision, to grant it the recognition and support that it deserves. There is a misguided shibboleth among the so-called advisers of central government that it is not the successes of the English language that need support, but the failures. This is like telling a farmer to stop feeding the cows that are milking and give their food to those that are not. This attitude is crass, ill-informed and sentimental. To support the English language is to support a resource as vital and fundamental to our country as fossil fuels are to the City of London.

The most sensible, efficient and certainly the cheapest way such support can be achieved is to accept that books are indeed different. And to leave them firmly zero-rated.

Any other way would not only be, in the time honoured phrase, a tax on knowledge, but would be precisely, and almost by definition, a piece of penny pinching and pernicious censorship. Even for this reason alone any such taxation proposal should be opposed.

Acknowledgements

I am indebted to the following for their help in the preparation of this article:
The Publishers' Association
Fergus Dunlop
Dr Derek Morris
Dr John Vickers
The Booksellers' Association
Peggy Bowyer

Notes

1. Department of Education and Science.
2. Publishers' Association: Book Trade Yearbook 1987.
3. *The Times*, 18 April 1988.

5 The Predators' Press

Tom Baistow

It is a measure of Mrs Thatcher's much-vaunted free-for-all philosophy, with unfettered competition as the route to ever-wider consumer choice, that under her regime three entrepreneurial predators, Rupert Murdoch, Robert Maxwell and Lord Stevens, are allowed to control no less than 77 per cent of Britain's uniquely dominant national press. To complete the paradox, the British, who read more newspapers than the citizens of any comparable country, and therefore should in theory be better informed than most, now largely read what in the last decade have become the trashiest, nastiest, most trivialised and politically biased tabloids in the world.

It has long been axiomatic that the real freedom of the British press is the freedom of millionaires to buy themselves newspapers that will propagate their personal views and promote their own ambitions, political and commercial. But at least in the past there was a diversity among press barons (several second generation) and a modifying minority of other owners – family trusts (*News Chronicle, Observer*) joint-control as in the TUC–Odhams *Daily Herald*, and the autonomous company-owned pre-Maxwell Mirror Group – that made for a more heterogeneous and responsible national press in terms of both editorial standards and political balance.

Today the concentration of ownership has reached near-monopoly and a new breed of brash tycoon has moved into the seats of editorial power. Five millionaires now own 15 of the 19 national titles, with 94 per cent of the daily market and 95 per cent of Sunday sales; but it is the three men who have risen to commercial power in the wheeler-dealer world of the takeover who have cornered the lion's share. Murdoch, Maxwell and Stevens are, in the final analysis, the editors-in-chief of much of what the nation reads (see Table 5.1).

All editing is, in effect, a form of censorship. In the case of newspapers it has become a continuous and all-pervasive censorship that poses a more fundamental and more effective threat to the free flow of untainted information than the Conservative Government's obsessive secrecy, as exemplified by its use of the Official Secrets Act and related injunctions against the *Guardian*, *Observer* and *Sunday Times* in its farcical attempts to bolt the *Spycatcher* stable door.

Newspaper proprietors appoint editors who, in the daunting task of

53

Table 5.1   Who owns what (press ownership)?

Total sales, national dailies and Sundays: 32 444 710

Murdoch	*Sun*	4 098 234		
	The Times	449 531		
	News of the World	5 151 794		
	Sunday Times	1 306 841		
	Today	350 257		
		11 356 657	=	35%
Maxwell	*Mirror*	3 087 512		
	Sunday Mirror	2 797 279		
	The People	2 766 126		
		8 650 917	=	26.6%
Stevens	*Daily Express*	1 690 538		
	Star	1 041 648		
	Sunday Express	2 193 746		
		4 925 932	=	15.1%
Rothermere	*Daily Mail*	1 800 539		
	Mail on Sunday	1 912 759		
		3 713 298	=	11.4%
Black	*Daily Telegraph*	1 154 018		
	Sunday Telegraph	730 674		
		1 884 692	=	5.8%
	Total	30 531 496	=	93.9%

Note: These figures are for the six-monthly period ending March 1988

increasing sales, will always toe the boss's line, know what to put in and what to keep out. Or, if it can't be kept out, how to angle it, or distort it, in the interests of house policy. The new concept of editorial independence was defined memorably by Victor (now Lord) Matthews when Trafalgar House took over the Beaverbrook Express in 1977: 'By and large, the editors will have complete freedom as long as they agree with the policy I have laid down'.

In a healthy democracy, with a truly representative range of media, both print and broadcasting, it is an aspect of implicit censorship that is offset and balanced for the readers by plurality of choice. But no longer in Britain. The traditional role of the press as the Fourth Estate, defender of the public interest, has been privatised with a vengeance. So what, apart from their conglomerate chequebooks and boundless professional acquisitiveness, are the qualities that qualify these self-appointed censors of news and views? Their careers and methods hardly mark them out as the disinterested guardians of the ark of editorial freedom and independence which a well-ordered society might choose to keep itself properly informed of the complex issues, domestic and international, that face an electorate in a rapidly changing world.

Two of them have controversial business reputations which seemed to have been largely forgotten in the predator-friendly climate created by Thatcherism. Maxwell (Mirror Group and a worldwide array of enterprises) was described by a Department of Trade inspector after a 1970s merger investigation as 'not a person who can be relied upon to exercise proper stewardship of a publicly quoted company'. 'Tiny' Rowland (*Observer* and 18 Scottish papers) heads Lonrho, whose activities during the same period were condemned by Edward Heath, then Prime Minister, as 'the unpleasant and unacceptable face of capitalism'.

Two are foreigners who run their commercial empires from abroad. Murdoch, Australian turned American, architect of a giant conglomerate controlling everything from a 75 per cent share of the Australian press, TV stations from Sydney to California, mining and airline interests, to book publishing and cinema chains, owns no fewer than five British national papers. Conrad Black, a Canadian newspaper publisher who 'rescued' the two *Telegraphs* from collapse and then took them over from Lord Hartwell, has recently bought the *Spectator*, the 160-year-old 'independent' weekly, from the Australian Fairfax chain.

Two whose papers are the most stridently 'patriotic' of all the Union Jack-waving nationals prefer to site their holding organisations outside British jurisdiction. Maxwell ('Forward with Britain') bases his parent foundation in Liechtenstein; and Viscount Rothermere, heir to his great-uncle Northcliffe, and a tax exile in France, failed in his attempt in 1988 to transfer the family's *Daily Mail* and General Trust plc to Holland to avoid £24m capital gains tax when the move was vetoed by the European Court of Justice.

One, Lord Stevens (Express Group of three nationals, 47 local papers and *Punch*, another 'independent' weekly) is an investment banker who came late into the newspaper industry to look after a City stake in United Newspapers' provincial chain before ousting Lord Matthews from the Express Group in a bitter, hostile takeover battle in 1985 that was crowned with one of Mrs Thatcher's entrepreneurial peerages. So far, Lord Stevens's most notable contribution to journalism was the grafting of *Sunday Sport*-type soft porn on to the sickly *Star*; a sortie into the gutter which provoked staff protests and ended only when its most important advertisers withdrew their custom in disgust – a rare example of market forces putting ethics first.

All are men of the Right with the idiosyncratic exception of Maxwell, a former Labour MP who combines the clout of a heavyweight capitalist with asseverations of socialist faith.

It is to Murdoch, however, that the discredit must go for the British press's deplorable slide into junk journalism. When he bought the *Sun* (né *Daily Herald*) for a song from IPC (the Mirror Group writ large) in 1969 he turned the intelligent middle-rank popular broadsheet overnight into a salacious tabloid. What had been Labour's own daily a few years before was transmogrified into a sex and crime magazine, plus Page Three nipples, which attracted a significant new readership whose staple diet until then had been the teenage comic. Within the decade Murdoch's cynical formula had generated a circulation of over 4 million, demoralised and overtaken the once-great *Mirror* and panicked the rest of the struggling populars into the (mistaken) conclusion that what one might call down-market forces were the cure for Fleet Street's financial malaise.

Murdoch's formula was to narrow the whole editorial focus. Crime and sex scandals had always been an ingredient of both quality and popular papers (no paper devoted more space to these human failings than the *Daily Telegraph*, which sanitised them for suburban consumption with muted typography). But two factors kept such topics in reasonable proportion. For one thing, the sheer size of the traditional broadsheet meant that 'spicy' stories were only a minor part of the wide coverage of home and foreign news of all kinds, both heavy and light. For another, sex and crime were reported only when they broke through the courts. Even the *News of the World* – known in the trade as Screws of the World before Murdoch was born – relied largely on criminal and divorce proceedings for its staple copy, presented in deadpan detail.

The spectacular circulation success of his sleazy *Sun* changed all that. Within the last decade every popular broadsheet except for the *Sunday Express* has turned tabloid and moved downmarket in varying degrees in the intensifying battle for readers. The long-endemic circulation war had been stepped up by the post-OPEC recession's blow to advertising revenue and the continuing rise in labour costs (about which more later). A switch to tabloid size seemed to be the sovereign remedy for all Fleet Street's ills, particularly the ad famine: a full page, although only half the broadsheet size, still commanded relatively high rates and cut dollar-priced newsprint bills by enabling papers to palm off the readers with, say, a 36-page issue which was in fact the equivalent of only 18 pages of the old broadsheet.

Editorially, this managerial con trick was complemented by the changeover to brash tabloid typography that has fundamentally altered the character of popular journalism. The broadsheet, however 'pop', was essentially a text paper: the average page contained some 4000 words – enough to develop detailed reports, offering readers coverage of a wide selection catering for varying tastes within the same paper and providing them with a more or less balanced three-dimensional picture of the world, despite any individual house bias.

In the downmarket tabloid the packaging has become at least as important as the content: massive monosyllabic headlines and huge pictures which leave space for barely 700–800 words on an inside page – more often a mere 200 on the front itself. It is a format which offers a degree of oversimplification ideally suited to the dramatisation of the trivial and the sordid into the sensational and the reduction of political coverage to biased hype or personal smear. News editing – world shattering events apart – has been narrowed down and perverted to feed the formula. Complicated, important social issues take up too much space. Even courtroom sensations are no longer enough: today's tabloid reporters sniff out 'exclusive' scandals, trailing public figures and showbiz 'celebrities' like private eyes bribing anyone from friends and servants to prostitutes and criminals for the dirt that crowds the real news into ten-line paragraphs on page nine.

Chequebook journalism has long been a standby of popular Sundays with flagging sales, ritually condemned by the impotent Press Council, subsiding and surfacing again in an increasingly vicious cycle. But the watershed came in 1981 after the arrest of the 'Yorkshire Ripper', when the uninhibited pursuit of sensational copy at any price, financial or metaphorical, in frenzied competition for every gory, lubricious detail of Peter Sutcliffe's trail of bloody sex murders provoked the Press Council into publishing an 80 000 word indictment of 'lynch-mob journalism'.

That denunciation, like the Council's Declaration of Principles condemning chequebook methods and intrusions into privacy that were not in the public interest, has been contemptuously ignored or aggressively attacked by the tabloids. The Press Council's latest annual report records 1269 complaints, a 12 per cent increase over the year. The flood of protests about misrepresentation and mistreatment by the press has soared by 300 per cent in 20 years. And, significantly, nearly 40 per cent of the complaints upheld over the years concern the failure of papers to publish replies and corrections, or the alterations made to readers' letters to fudge their complaints before publication. It will be seen from the accompanying table (table 5.2) that right-wing papers fill the top half of both categories, with Murdoch's two tabloids in leading positions.

Table 5.2   Complaints upheld by the Press Council over 17 years, 1969–1986

Dailies		Sundays	
Daily Mail	48	News of the World	24
Sun	38	Sunday Times	16
Daily Express	37	Sunday Express	14
Daily Telegraph	27	Mail on Sunday	13
The Times	18	Observer	8
Star	14	People	7
Mirror	13	Sunday Telegraph	5
Guardian	11	Sunday Mirror	1
Today	2		

Source: Press Council annual reports.

Note: Two papers have been publishing for a relatively short period – *Mail on Sunday* (1982) and *Today* (1986).

As controversial as the new breed of proprietors themselves are the circumstances in which three of them acquired their papers. Murdoch, a small-time Australian publisher with little real money of his own but limitless ambition and *chutzpah* to match, flew into London in 1969 to play the white knight who would save Sir Emsley Carr's giant but ailing *News of the World* from a takeover bid by the Czech-born Maxwell and keep it, in the then editor's memorable phrase, 'as English as roast beef'. Within months Murdoch had secretly bought up a controlling stake with borrowed funds, adroitly separated the bemused Sir Emsley from his dubious patrimony and taken over his chair. The deal which secured the sinking *Sun* from the new IPC boss, Hugh (now Lord) Cudlipp, eager to be rid of what not so long before had been 'the Voice of Labour', was a pushover. It was made memorable only by Murdoch's blunt refusal to renew the pledge, given by Cecil King when he had bought out the Odhams group in 1961, that the paper would continue to keep faith with its Labour tradition.

After 13 years in which the *Sun* and *News of the World* had pioneered new lows in popular journalism, Murdoch engineered his biggest raid. *The Times* and its sister *Sunday Times* had been put up for sale after the disastrous year-long stoppage brought about by a combination of managerial bullying and stupidity and union myopia and intransigence. The record of his two papers, condemned by the Press Council and an outraged Establishment, made it unthinkable that Murdoch would be allowed to get his hands on these twin pillars of journalistic probity, even if their owner, Toronto-based Kenneth Thomson, son of Roy, was happy with the deal. It would never get past the Monopolies and Mergers Commission.

But, true to form, Mrs Thatcher was undismayed by the unthinkable. What if Murdoch's two papers were nasty rags, the very antithesis of those prized Victorian values? Had they not rivalled even the *Mail* and *Express* in their Labour-baiting and union-bashing line in 1979, contributing their own brand of venom to the campaign that had brought her to power? After all, their combined readership of some 25 million, overwhelmingly working class, is an ideal audience for her populism. Mr Murdoch is indeed an invaluable ally. Within three days her then Trade Secretary, John Biffen, had decided that one man's ownership of four national papers was hardly a case for the Commission and approved the takeover.

That was not to be the government's last acknowledgement of Murdoch's valuable support. When Eddy Shah's imaginative, all-electronic but undercapitalised *Today* ran out of money in 1986, six months after its much-hyped launch, 'Tiny' Rowland came to the rescue with an injection of cash. But after a year of continuing drain he decided to cut Lonrho's losses. A familiar white knight was waiting in the wings – Rupert Murdoch, with a cheque for £38m in one hand and an ultimatum in the other: unless he got clearance from the Trade Secretary the following day the 'rescue' was off and the paper would fold. Lord Young waived even a token reference to the Monopolies Commission, and Murdoch, incredibly, had added a fifth paper to his national stable. To rub in the nature of his victory, he appointed as editor the man who had been in charge of the *News of the World*.

Murdoch may not be finished yet in his quest for the perfect personal monopoly. His next target could be Pearson, the huge group which owns the *Financial Times* and 29 local papers as well as a conglomerate ranging from Lazard's merchant bank to Madame Tussaud's. Already he has increased his stake to 20 per cent. If he raises this to 25 per cent he will face the possibility of reference to the Monopolies Commission. It is a less than daunting possibility: the prospect of Murdoch imposing his ultra-Thatcherite views on the admirably fair and objective *FT* would be balm to No. 10, even if, for appearance's sake, he had to give up *The Times* to get hold of the City's bible.

Back to 1981 and another curious case involving a paper almost as old as, and in many ways more distinguished than, *The Times*. The Astor family (itself of American origin) had in 1976 given up the fight to stem the long-running losses of the *Observer* (in no small part due to union behaviour) and handed over the venerable (1791) Sunday paper, much admired for the quality of its liberal journalism, to Atlantic Richfield, a Los Angeles oil company, for a virtual peppercorn. The real price for Arco was that its chairman, Robert O. Anderson, a philanthropist with a highly publicised social conscience, would guarantee a 'long and illustrious future' for the paper. Five years into that illustrious future, in February 1981, Anderson cut Arco's £8m losses and handed over control, in a secret deal worth some £6m to 'Tiny' Rowland, the international entrepreneur who not so long ago had provoked Edward Heath's moral wrath.

To head off any government intervention that might cancel the backstairs coup, Anderson and Rowland changed the terms of the deal. But this time the storm of criticism forced Mrs Thatcher's hand and the case went before the Commission. Predictably, however, Biffen approved the takeover.

The next big sell-out, this time of the only three nationals which support Labour – however half-heartedly – was a classic case of the shareholder-bribing technique that is the mainspring of the entrepreneurial ethos. When Reed International, the cuckoo that had itself taken over IPC, decided in October 1983 to get rid of Mirror Group Newspapers – three nationals, two Scottish papers and *Sporting Life*

– its chairman, Sir Alex Jarratt, declared that to safeguard their 'traditions and character and editorial independence' the share capital would be distributed among a large number of ordinary shareholders to keep predators at bay; no single offer from one individual would be entertained, and an independent chairman acceptable to City institutions would be appointed. Clive Thornton, who had masterminded the Alliance Building Society's success, got the job. As an earnest of its intentions, Reed turned down an offer of £100m from a consortium of MGN editorial–managerial staff, backed by merchant banks, because it said it was determined that the papers should not fall into the hands of any one group, even its own journalists.

But there was one predator who knew that even the highest minded capitalists have their price. If ever one man could be said to need his own newspaper it was Robert Maxwell, spectacularly successful in the takeover league but still trying to live down his once seemingly tarnished City reputation. Ever since Murdoch had snatched the *News of the World* from under his nose he had been a failed bidder at a number of Fleet Street auctions. This time the City, ironically, was on his side – however accidentally. The big financial institutions turned down Thornton's commendable multiple-share structure, devised to block any takeover; for them editorial independence was plainly not a marketable commodity.

Maxwell moved in with a cheque for £80m. Jarratt repeated his pledge and rejected the bid. Delving deeper into his overdraft, Maxwell produced a bigger cheque, this time for £113m and a shrewd line of bait aimed at the Reed board, looking anxiously over its shoulder at its shareholders: 'I cannot see how it can turn down more cash on the table than it would receive through the market.' The extra £33m overcame the last of Reed's scruples.

Next day Maxwell marched into the *Mirror* building in Holborn and declared: 'I am the proprietor, 100 per cent. There can be only one boss and that's me.' To rub in the full import of his coup, he added: 'The cash in MGN, its shareholding in Reuters and the building together are equal to what I paid for it. The papers are in for free.' The papers were also in for an exercise in personality cult, starting with Maxwell conducting his editors round Britain in a special train to 'find out what the readers really want'.

To be fair, however, Maxwell has kept his promise that the papers would 'fight for the return of a Labour government', however qualified in relation to Labour's key policies.

THE FIFTH ESTATE

Not all the manipulation of the press is as transparent as the more bizarre antics and self-interested campaigns of some of its overlords. So far as the newspaper reader is concerned, censorship comes stealthily in more than one guise. Not the least insidious is that practised by the booming public relations industry in insinuating its 'product', as it likes to call it, into almost every page of the paper; from the editorial matter plugging consumer goods advertised in adjoining columns to the less easily identifiable, and therefore more sinister, projection of commercial and political ideas and attitudes and views disguised as news. Everyone from the Prime Minister to the latest rock star's agent, and, not least, big business, has something to sell.

Basically, the aim of PR is the same as that of the newspaper owner: to tell you what it wants you to know and keep out of print what it would rather you didn't know. Today there are probably more than half as many 'practitioners' as there are journalists in what I have called elsewhere the Fifth Estate. They come in all shapes and sizes: small one-desk firms infiltrating their puffs into local papers; large in-house teams of major companies with both product and industrial relations axes to grind; international groups which lay on 'freebies' – all-expenses-paid trips with lavish hospitality designed to put moral pressure on journalists to write friendly pieces about the client's activities and policies – not infrequently to describe the humane and happy conditions of life in barbarous regimes such as that of South Africa. By no means least, there is the 1000-strong army of Whitehall information officers putting out the government's version of the state of the nation from the official gloss on the latest economic or unemployment figures to the PM's views on anything that might inspire a favourable headline.

At the apex of the Whitehall information pyramid is the Prime Minister's press secretary, Bernard Ingham, a former journalist, whose zealous efforts on the PM's behalf have inspired widespread criticism that No. 10's use of news management techniques has bordered on the unethical. The main instrument of news management is the unattributable briefing of lobby correspondents. The fact that these secret briefings can only be quoted obliquely under the 'well-informed sources' device make them an ideal medium for planting the government version of political events, flying kites that can later be denied, and putting the boot in against Opposition leaders – or even a member of the government who has got out of line.

Socialist criticism that Ingham is more Thatcherite than the Prime Minister herself should be tempered by the realisation that it was the Attlee government which first appointed a public relations adviser who was a professional journalist rather than the traditional civil servant – Francis Williams, a former editor of the *Daily Herald*, who was later made a life peer. Harold Wilson followed suit by appointing as his press secretary Joe Haines, also a former *Daily Herald* journalist, a Labour activist now on the *Mirror*, and biographer of Maxwell. It was the Wilson–Haines partnership which pioneered the now-familiar ploy of contrived interviews and 'photo opportunities' that can boost the prime ministerial image or, by shrewd timing, steal the Opposition's thunder by diverting media attention at crucial junctures. Today Mrs Thatcher has added a further, commercial dimension to the art of fooling a lot of the people some of the time, or at least taking their eyes off the ball, by hiring outside consultants and advertising experts like Saatchi to market her like an American presidential candidate.

In the age of high-powered hype it would be Canute-like to try to stem the waves of carefully generated Downing Street publicity which most of an uncritical supine press is happy to swallow whole for the good of its favourite party. But at least a reforming administration could tackle the conspiracy of the anonymous Lobby system. Ideally, prime ministers would hold regular and open press conferences on the White House model, with questions and answers on the record, although Parliament's jealous protection of its traditional right to hear all government policy statements first could prove an obvious stumbling block. If that proves insurmountable, the system should be scrapped. To their credit, the *Independent* and *Guardian* have shown the way by boycotting the loaded Lobby briefings in favour of digging – with notable success – for their 'inside' political news.

THE UNIONS' ROLE

At this point it has to be said that the corrupting cynicism which can spring from untrammelled power is not the monopoly of the new press barons. The erosion of editorial ethics and standards by self-interested proprietors and complaisant journalists was paralleled for 30 years by an equally self-interested distortion of the economics of production by a Fleet Street workforce that played its part in creating the conditions of decline which paved the way to Wapping. Underlying the distortion was a hidden element of censorship: papers which delighted in exposing the malpractices of other – preferably nationalised – industries ('Car workers sleep away the night shift!') remained mute about the anarchy in their own production departments for fear that the union chapels would counter with costly stoppages.

To be sure it was that archetypal press baron, Lord Beaverbrook himself, who started it all by inventing the notorious 'ghost workers' in the 1950s to get round the *Daily Express* machine-room chapels' limit on the number of copies they allowed each press unit to print and, at the same time, weaken less profitable rival papers. As the crafty Beaver knew, the crews were only too happy to ignore their own protective rules in return for the shared-out real-life wage packets of their mythical mates. When Mickey Mouse joined the press-room payroll he instituted the 'Old Spanish customs' which were ultimately to deliver a spectacularly overpaid and overstaffed workforce into Rupert Murdoch's hands.

The numerous, virtually autonomous chapels (department branches) of the two main unions, the National Graphical Association, representing the typesetters and allied craft workers, and SOGAT, which organises the machine room and distribution sides, had for years forced weak and inefficient managements into costly pay settlements by threatening stoppages. These stoppages could – and did – drive papers into the red unless they paid up. During the post-OPEC advertising famine the loss of millions of copies cost papers dear. Unmoved by the endemic financial crisis, the chapels refused to introduce the 'new' (26-year-old) technology except on their own terms, ignoring – and more than once booing – the attempts of their more far-sighted national leaders to clean up the most blatant ramps and rationalise the long-outmoded and discredited wage and manpower structure. The two unions' provincial members were already coming to terms with electronic printing, but for Fleet Street linotype operators who could get £25 000–£50 000 a year for tapping a keyboard and SOGAT machine men £16 000 for in effect a two-day week, plus another two days' shifts on other papers, the goose that had laid ever-bigger golden eggs, virtually on demand, was not to be sacrificed in the name of either progress or company profits.

By the start of the 1970s several papers had planned to outmanoeuvre the chapels by transferring their main production plants to 'greenfield' sites in Docklands. By moving three miles down river they hoped to enter the age of computerised printing and slash manning levels at one go. Murdoch was the first to get his riverside printworks ready for action, but in 1985, after two years of negotiation it still lay empty, eating its head off in interest charges. The unions would not budge except on their terms, which did not include the job losses implicit in the switch to new technology. On the face of things, the catalyst was the maverick Eddy Shah, the Lancashire free-sheet printer who had bested the NGA in a legal battle over the closed shop and was now setting up his revolutionary new daily, *Today*, totally computerised, with journalists setting their own copy, its presses and machines manned by only one union. In return for its monopoly, the EETPU had signed a no-strike agreement. Significantly, however, it was Andrew Neil, editor of Murdoch's *Sunday Times*, who had some time earlier suggested to Shah that he could outflank both Fleet Street and its unions by launching a new national paper from a greenfield site free from all traditional chapel power. Murdoch's plot had been deeply laid.

By December 1985 he was ready to spring the trap. Having secretly trained a small team of imported electricians at the new Wapping plant, turned it into a barbed-wire protected fortress and checked that he could legally dismiss a striking workforce without compensation, he issued his shotgun ultimatum: give me a Shah-type deal by Christmas or else... Both NGA and SOGAT chapels fell for his ploy; they decided to strike after the now statutory ballot. Confident of their clout, they cocked a snook at Murdoch by basing their ballot on the claim that their members should be guaranteed their jobs for life. Plainly they believed they could force him back to the negotiating table by keeping his two profitable tabloids off the news-stands. They had failed to realise that an Australian who gladly adopts American citizenship to get his hands on a US television network means business in the most ruthless sense of that phrase.

The rest is history. The moonlight flit to Wapping, the overnight sacking of 5500 and the siege of the fortress that followed brought no credit to either side or to the police in the middle of the year-long dispute. Brutal as the outcome was for the families of the sacked, the genesis of the whole tragic affair – and it gives a socialist no pleasure to say so – was much of the chapels' own making, the bitter fruit of greed and arrogance and a sectarian selfishness that betrayed the collective principles of honest trade unionism.

Since the traumatic events of 1986 the Wapping tide has swept
Fleet Street off the publishing map, as the other papers, emboldened
by Murdoch's strong-arm tactics, have bought out another 5000 jobs
and moved to their own greenfield sites as far apart as Battersea and
the Isle of Dogs. Today the Wapping revolution is virtually complete,
as journalists man the keyboards the NGA fought so fiercely to
retain. The total wage bill has been cut by more than £100m and for
the first time in years, with advertising booming, newspapers are
again making real money. The annual profits of Murdoch's five
British papers soared last year by £99m to a total of £111.5m. That is
no cash bonus for Britain: the millions he is making, largely from the
Sun, *News of the World* and *Sunday Times*, are helping to fund his
satellite TV channels and stemming the heavy losses of his Fox TV
and cinema chains for which he swopped his Australian birthright.

As the press's profits rise, the standards of the tabloids sink in inverse
ratio to the ever fiercer battle for sales. Behind the frenetic competition
is the unblinkable fact that the total sales of the populars have continued
to decline since the peak in the 1960s: a million less in the case of the
dailies, seven million less for the Sundays. Mass circulations became
essential to attract the advertising that paid production costs, inflated
out of all proportion to sales revenue by inordinate wage bills. Yet
today, with the wage bill cut by over a third, there has been no let-up in
the slide down market. If yesterday's excesses were committed in the
interests of survival, today's are in the interests of bigger profits.

It is a gloomy picture, relieved only by the launch and success, in
barely two years, of the excellent new quality daily the *Independent*.
The significance of its breakthrough is that it was founded by a
journalist, Andreas Whittam Smith, and a group of editorial colleagues who raised £18m in the City and have already repaid half the
launch capital, and that its share structure is designed to keep
predators at bay. The paper is well named: here is the prototype of a
new class of independent papers which could emerge in the more
rational economic conditions of the post-Wapping age and bring back
the diversity essential to a truly free and democratic press. But first a
future government will have to tackle the millionaires' near monopoly
at its roots, about which more later.

NEW LAWS FOR OLD

The irony of the tradition that newspapers must be free, in the words
of the 1977 Royal Commission on the Press, to act as 'watchdogs for

citizens by scrutinising concentrations of power', is that the press itself has become just such a concentration of power – personal power exercised by men who control both massive commercial empires and the very instruments of scrutiny themselves. To give just one example: newspapers belonging to both Maxwell and Murdoch have opposed increases in the BBC licence fee. They also extol the virtues of satellite television, in which both now have commercial stakes.

Unlike its contemporaries in the United States and most European countries, the British press is hedged in by a thicket of legal constraints that have conspired with the self-interest of proprietors to tame the will to disclose, without fear or favour, that is the bedrock of serious journalism. The almost paranoiac passion for secrecy which marks the Thatcher government has worsened the situation, but the most effective censorship of revelations that may demonstrably be in the public interest has long derived from our antiquated and punitive libel and contempt laws.

Together they form a formidable barrier to real investigative journalism. Fear of an action for defamation which can cost a paper the better part of £1m in damages and costs makes most editors reach for the spike. Similarly, 'gagging' injunctions secured under the contempt laws can keep a public scandal out of the public prints for years, as in the *Sunday Times*'s long campaign to be allowed to expose the thalidomide tragedy.

If our national press is ever to fulfil its proper role as the public's watchdog, a future government will have to drag the law into line with the realities of modern life. First, it will need to introduce a Freedom of Information Act giving both press and public a statutory right of access to all official information that does not involve national defence or economic security (see chapter 8). In its turn the press will have to offer more than one *quid pro quo* to the public whose welfare it claims to defend. To balance its new right of access to official sources there would be a Privacy Bill to provide legal protection against intrusion into private lives where no question of the public interest – as distinct from the interest of a prurient public – was involved.

The second, and equally important, right that a reformed and responsible press would have to concede to the public is the Right of Reply, a common feature of press law in other countries which both Parliament and newspapers in Britain have consistently rejected. Twice in the last decade Parliament has thrown out Private Members'

Bills designed to provide a means of immediate redress to both
ordinary citizens and organisations claiming that they have been
seriously misreported, misrepresented or maligned by the media.
Both were introduced by Labour MPs: Frank Allaun, then Member
for East Salford, in 1982; and Ann Clwyd, Member for Cynon
Valley, early in 1988. Allaun's Bill proposed that replies to factually
inaccurate or distorted reports or comments should be printed within
three days by the editor concerned, in the same position and up to the
same length as the offending item. Complaints disputed by the editor
would be referred to a panel of judicial status, comprising representatives of the public, journalism, media management and the trade
unions, presided over by a judge. Where a complaint was upheld the
editor would be required to publish the reply within three days of
receiving the panel's judgment or be liable to a fine of between £2000
and £40 000, according to the seriousness of the offence.

Allaun's Bill had the merit of concentrating on the Right of Reply
alone (here I should declare my interest, having been involved in its
initiation). The weakness of Ms Clwyd's Bill was that it attempted to
do too much by proposing that legal aid should be extended to those
wishing to sue for libel. Inevitably, both were universally savaged by
both quality and popular newspapers. Their line was predictable: not
only would such an Act be an unacceptable interference with the
editor's independence (*sic*) but unworkable, as replies flooded in
from every crank in the country and filled up valuable editorial space
(*sic*).

This argument chooses to ignore the fact that Right of Reply laws
are administered in several European countries without infringing
press freedom. The most obvious example is West Germany, where
each Land has its own press legislation. The country's biggest popular
paper, *Bild*, with a circulation of over 5 million, prints some 50
'counter statements' from complainants each year – hardly the
avalanche British editors fear. If the Right of Reply can work
routinely without fuss in Germany and elsewhere, why is it such an
unthinkable concept in freedom-loving Britain? For if British editors
were not blinded by prejudice they would realise that an institutional
Right of Reply could have a valuable twofold effect. First it would
enlarge editorial freedom by limiting the libel risk, providing genuine
complainants with immediate, free redress in place of long, costly law
suits. Secondly, and not least, it would extend the democratic process
by opening such redress to ordinary people who cannot afford to
bring an action for defamation.

Britain is the only important Western country without a written constitution embodying laws which both guarantee the press's freedom and define its responsibilities. If our mass-circulation tabloids are ever to regain journalistic integrity and a representative plurality is to be restored, a future government – and it necessarily will have to be a socialist one – will face a formidable task. Not only will it have to bring in new legislation of the kind outlined above but draw up a charter establishing a legal framework for the internal reform of the press itself. This would have to be wide-ranging and based on a code of conduct to be enforced by a new Press Council, armed with power to impose real sanctions, such as substantial fines, on papers that deliberately or knowingly breach the rules. To obviate unnecessary resort to the Press Council, or Rights of Reply panel, each paper would have an ombudsman/woman on the US and Canadian model to deal with routine complaints. To ensure that editors are not simply proprietors' puppets to be hired and fired at will (the *Daily Express* has had five in the last eight years), the charter would specify two safeguards: firstly, machinery for the involvement of staff in their appointment, and secondly, inclusion on each board independent directors from outside the paper, to protect them from improper pressure from whatever sources. Ownership and control of newspapers, direct or indirect, would be restricted to persons of British nationality and companies or organisations whose controlling body is based and registered in the UK. (At present there is no reason why, say, one of the oil states could not through a covert agency take over a newspaper group and use it to promote its own Middle East and OPEC policies.)

Above all, the Monopolies and Mergers Commission's writ will have to be revised to conform to the realities of the post-Wapping press. In the past, the bizarre economics of Fleet Street meant that a proprietor could reasonably claim that he needed two, preferably three, national titles to rationalise production overheads, maximise the deployment of machines and workforce, to make his group potentially viable. Today, electronic publishing, with press runs rented at satellite print centres at strategic points throughout the country, as in the case of the *Independent*, has rendered that claim as obsolete as hot metal typesetting. Ironically, the technological revolution unleashed so brutally by Murdoch contains the key that could both shut out his kind of monopoly and open the door to a truly diverse press. Honesty demands the admission that when Mrs Thatcher has finally been forced to retreat to Dulwich *les Deux Églises* it will take a government of the left with real guts to turn that key.

6 Counter Culture and the Small Journal

Phil Kelly

Writers, journalists, editors and others who deal with the written word as a medium through which to describe the world, to analyse it, to inform, to inspire to warn, to excite, even to entertain or to amuse, are on the whole reluctant to admit that in a society and culture where any goods or services can be bought and sold, their own words too are commodities for sale.

There are probably over 5000 weekly and monthly periodicals produced and nationally distributed in Britain, most catering for a myriad of specialist interests, jobs and professions. About half, 2400, are 'consumer' magazines, directed at people's leisure interests, the others 'trade' publications, directed at work and professional concerns.

Increasingly, 'trade' publications are distributed directly by mail, either on paid subscriptions, or free to a list of subscribers whose occupation or profession will attract enough specialised advertising to cover their entire costs. But, for those relying on the newspaper and magazine distribution trade, broad shoulders and generous resources are a great advantage.

An article in *Magazine Week* (18 May 1988) by Tony Norris set out the realities of the periodical trade. Figures compiled by the Audit Bureau of Circulation show that only about 5 per cent of consumer titles sell over 100 000 copies per issue. The remainder sell between 5000 and 90 000 copies – an average of 32 000 copies.

That is less than one copy for each of the 38 000 to 40 000 retail outlets for magazines in Britain. 4000, mainly in rural areas, only operate rounds, delivering ordered publications to customers' homes. They do not have premises where people can walk in off the street and buy a publication on impulse.

Of the retail newsagents' shops, 24 000 are tiny corner-shop outlets, with room to display only a small selection of titles. A few hundred of the 12 000 larger shops, from branches of the multiple newsagents like W.H. Smith and John Menzies, through the larger shops belonging to the smaller chains, to the larger remaining independent newsagents, might display up to 1500 titles, though monthlies may appear on the shelves only in the week or fortnight after publication.

Among 'larger' shops, according to Norris, there is a sharp gradation by size. The major volume of sales comes through the branches of the retail chains owned by W.H. Smith and John Menzies. 'It is the prime locations – railway termini, airports and increasingly motorway service stations – which move the high volumes', he pointed out.

W.H. Smith lists 1500 titles in its stock list, but 350 to 400 titles would be a good display for an average outlet. The fact that any of the others can be ordered and supplied if the customer insists is no consolation for a small publisher seeking to expand circulation, and entirely rules out any spontaneous increase in circulation because of a sudden but perhaps temporary interest in a periodical.

This is particularly the case for a journal of political opinion like *Tribune*. Much attention has been directed in recent years to the falling sales, not only of *Tribune*, but of other journals of left opinion, analysis and comment, like the *New Statesman*.

A number of reasons have been advanced for the fall in circulation of the Left press. The growth of detailed analysis and informed comment in the Sunday press is one. More fundamentally, some commentators have sought to link it with their view that the radical social views espoused by such periodicals were no longer offering solutions to Britain's problems. Pointing up the falling circulations of Left papers has been an element in the New Right's attempt, successful even among some erstwhile radicals, to undermine the Left by convincing us that we suffer from a crisis of intellectual relevance.

The answer may be more simple. All periodicals suffer from circulation decay. When a former reader stops buying a paper, the newsagent, or branch manager, reduces the order by one. But when a casual potential reader seeks to buy a copy of a small circulation paper, it is unlikely to be there. This is particularly galling for a paper like *Tribune*, which fairly regularly gets a mention or a reference in other newspapers, or even on television; far more often than the other 2400 consumer magazines. Yet this increase in interest cannot be translated into increased sales.

Eight years ago, in their book *Where is the Other News?*, published by the Minority Press Group, Dave Berry, Liz Cooper and Charles Landry described the experiences of radical publishers trying to get their titles accepted by the High Street news trade.

'In order to keep a commercial magazine going, it needs to be promoted to a series of audiences,' they wrote. 'Readers, so that circulation is kept up; advertisers and advertising agencies, who judge a magazine's worth by its projected circulation within particular target audiences; newsagents and wholesalers, who predominantly stock magazines that are widely known.'

In other words, it is cash, not content, which has the larger impact on magazine circulations. Of course, magazines with large promotion budgets have failed; Sir James Goldsmith's *Now* is the most famous example. Magazines without large promotion budgets, like *Private Eye*, *Time Out*, and *Spare Rib*, have established themselves. But in general and in the long run, money talks.

Whether the newsagent is an independent or a branch of a chain, the pressure, as in all retail business, is to maximise turnover with minimum effort. For the newsagent, regular sales of high-circulation publications are the backbone of income for a trade faced with ever-rising rents. Since 1979 rates too have risen as central government has reduced support for local authorities and placed the burden of local public expenditure increasingly on local communities.

For existing publications, the struggle to maintain circulation, and for new ones, the battle to break in to the High Street, is the publishers' principal concern.

All new periodicals face the challenge of acceptance by the news trade. For periodicals which are left-wing, radical, or otherwise unconventional in the views they represent, the task is doubly difficult. Although they claim not to, the main wholesale distribution chains, W.H. Smith, John Menzies and the smaller Surridge Dawson, 'the big 2½', operate what is effectively a form of political censorship.

This censorship is not any less oppressive in fact because the distribution trade genuinely does not believe that its practices amount to censorship. Censorship is generally understood in our society to signify political, non-commercial considerations, brought into play, either by state authority, or extra-legal non-state power, to interfere with the content of publications or their general availability.

Of course there is also state censorship in Britain. It is underpinned by the Official Secrets Act, soon to be strengthened if the present government has its way, but extends to the day-to-day practice of government in Britain. It is justified mainly on grounds of 'national security', and its harshest effect is on the reporting of military and intelligence matters. But that is a tautology; no state gives any reason for censorship other than to protect itself and its society.

The distribution of periodicals in Britain reflects a culture seeking to protect itself, to impose standards, and to suppress unorthodox views. It is part of the very fabric of social practice; commercial and financial considerations work with the grain of a social order searching for protection.

The crucial position of the 'big 2½' comes from their dominance of the trade. In the wholesale trade in England and Wales, 42 per cent of magazines are handled by W.H. Smith, 19 per cent by John Menzies and 8 per cent by Surridge Dawson. In Scotland, 93 per cent of all magazines are handled by John Menzies as wholesalers.

At the end of the 1970s, a number of radical publications came together to found the Publications Distribution Co-operative, in an attempt to find the collective commercial strength to challenge the commercial considerations cited by the major chains as the reason for their reluctance to handle alternative periodicals.

I was involved in the production of the *Leveller*, one of the publications which founded PDC. The co-operative's experience, recounted in *Where is the Other News?* was instructive:

All three big chains work closely together; it's very unlikely that any magazine which is acceptable to one is not acceptable to them all. However, Surridge Dawson has been known to take a magazine which others won't touch.

PDC took the *Leveller*, *Camerawork* (a radical photography magazine) and *Undercurrents* (a radical monthly on the environment) to the news manager at Smith's. He turned down *Undercurrents* and *Camerawork* without any discussion, but was prepared to look at the *Leveller*.

His tone, however, was very discouraging, pointing out that 'this wasn't quite Smith's' and 'you can probably do that better yourselves'. When pushed, he spoke of a 15 000 circulation as the minimum Smith's would look at before being interested. (The *Leveller* print run at that time was 6000.) He also referred to the trial of *Socialist Challenge* [the weekly produced by the Trotskyist International Marxist Group], commenting that the paper wasn't selling very well. (About 300 copies of *Socialist Challenge* were taken by Smith's for a trial period of about a year in some London outlets.)

So, the news manager suggested, Smith's were already covering the area of radical politics. But he didn't say he would turn down the *Leveller* because of its radical content. His concern, he said, was for the economic viability of the product because of the lack of advertising, its ability to appear regularly, and its overall appearance. He also had doubts as to who would be the audience. He didn't think it would sell.

He thought it over for a few days, but the answer was no. John Menzies turned down PDC titles because they were 'looking for a more professional product, national advertising, and "repping" by the publisher' – i.e. direct approaches to encourage retailers to stock and display the magazines. This is beyond the resources not only of radical publishers, but also of small-circulation consumer periodicals which do get distributed.

Surridge Dawson accepted the titles. But in the first issue of *Undercurrents* which had been distributed to a number of local branches, an article on 'Growing your own dope' appeared. The result of this was a directive from head office not to accept any further material from the distributors of *Undercurrents*. This meant that Surridge Dawson not only threw out the magazine containing the 'offending' article, but also rejected the *Leveller* and *Camerawork*, which not only had nothing to do with the problem, but had been accepted by a number of local branches and were selling well.

In general, the authors of *Where is the Other News?* say, when publishers of new radical magazines approach the big wholesale distributors to ask what they must do to have their title accepted, 'You are given a guided tour through the complexities of advertising, publicity and promotion, the distribution trade, unionisation and labour problems, British Rail, professionalisation, the media etc, etc. Actually, what they are saying is "no, it is too political. It's too left wing. It will upset the family image".'

Of course, the consumer magazine market is far from static. Big publishers are constantly seeking new titles. One company which has grown over the past decade is EMAP National Publishers, which has grown out of the strong regional and local newspaper base of its owners, East Midlands Allied Press. More recently, as trading and investment across national boundaries in the European Community has become more common, German, Dutch and French publishers have launched magazines aimed at the women's market, often in collaboration with British publishers.

Big publishers have the resources to research a market, and to produce a magazine aimed carefully at a particular income group, age range, and set of consumption patterns, usually dignified with the title 'lifestyle'. It is not only the readers who are assiduously researched. One of the stiffest tests is the presentation of proposals for a magazine, typically also with 'dummy' issues, to advertising agencies. Consumer magazines do not survive without the support of the major advertisers.

Publishers are happy to consider ideas from outsiders, but they go through the same research mill. From the point of view of the reader, the result is more of the same. One computer magazine, one women's magazine, one home decorating magazine, looks much like another. Magazines fold, often because their readers' tastes change, particularly in the women's market, or as the hobbies they write about, such as home movies or the first home computers, are eclipsed by new ones – video or more advanced machines. But the overall focus remains, and it is directed almost without exception at alternative ways of consuming.

Two titles which have been unsuccessfully launched in recent years, the right-of-centre weekly news magazine *Now*, and the left-inclined *News on Sunday* suffered from a lack of focus on a target market. *News on Sunday*'s failure was a particular blow for the British left. In their book *Disaster – the Rise and Fall of News on Sunday*, Chris Horrie and Peter Chippendale, former *NoS* journalists, describe the conflicts between the NoS's founders, journalists, and business staff.

One of the results was that insufficient was spent on promotion, and that the paper had no clear idea about which interests of which people it was addressing. So it lurched from one style and approach to another, an uncertainty which was reflected in the varying design of the paper itself, almost from week to week.

NoS was launched on favourable predictions from disinterested professionals on its potential for attracting readers and advertisers. Yet when it folded, under 18 per cent of potential readers were aware that it existed. The £6.5 million which *NoS* had was not enough to tell people about itself, and the vagaries of the product alienated many who actually found out about it.

In the past quarter of a century, successful magazines which have made it without the backing of a large group are to be counted on the fingers of one hand.

Private Eye started in the 1960s, a very different political and cultural age. It rose to its present circulation without any help from 'the big 2½'. Major wholesalers, and the big retail chains, refused to stock it for years. But its offer of apparently restricted knowledge, and its ability to persuade readers that they were becoming temporary members of an otherwise exclusive elite circle of political and business insiders, was an effective selling point. Coupled with its minimal production costs, it survived to become a best seller.

Time Out offered comprehensive information about popular cultural activity, which was, when it appeared, a unique service, albeit only to Londoners. Its radical politics, now only a memory, rode uneasily with yet another guide to different ways of consuming, and it now has no evident political position. *Time Out* too established its economic strength on the back of many years of low overheads and pay levels below those of other magazines.

Spare Rib, the pioneering feminist monthly, likewise survived by the effective self-exploitation of successive groups of women who produced it, coupled with the loyalty of readers to whom it offered coverage to be found nowhere else in the media. Its circulation is still far below that of consumption-oriented 'women's' magazines.

Three swallows in 25 years do not make a summer. These magazines made it, not with the help of the distribution and advertising industries, but because they managed to jump the hurdles which those industries, whose principal concern is guaranteed profit in the short term, place in the path of out-of-the-ordinary publications. As *Where is the Other News?* describes, financial considerations and an overriding insistence on normality mean that distribution arrangements in Britain stifle alternative views.

Tribune hovers ever uneasily between breakthrough and disappearance. 'The big 2½' would not stop distributing the paper, although its sales through the news trade are far smaller than they would demand for any new title. Tradition dies hard, and, even in Thatcher's Britain, *Tribune*'s political standpoint is still accepted as an integral part of the system of parliamentary democracy.

Half the Parliamentary Labour Party are members of the Tribune Group, which was founded as a parliamentary expression of the views which the paper supports – although the paper is independent of the group. If *Tribune* were to be refused distribution, there would be a justified outcry. But the major wholesale chains have made it clear that continued distribution is all we can expect.

In the boardrooms of the major chains, magazines are considered another product, like fridges, or holidays and leisure goods – of which W.H. Smith is now also a major distributor. Active intervention to promote an alternative view to that expressed in the majority of political publications is not their concern. In a politically pluralist society, the structure of magazine distribution is a major factor in keeping the printed media significantly less diverse than the political views of the population.

PDC collapsed in the early 1980s. The unequal struggle against the major distribution chains proved too great. PDC also serviced 'alternative' bookshops and non-traditional outlets, such as whole food shops, with radical and alternative publications. The alternative bookshops felt the pinch as the 1970s ebbed away and the culture which had supported them broke up.

Several left-wing publishers turned in the 1980s to smaller commercial distribution companies, which not only supply the big chains, but deliver to smaller wholesalers, and have the resources to 'rep' their titles, calling on the wholesalers and selected larger retail shops to encourage them to stock and display publications.

Marxism Today uses Magnum, as did *Labour Weekly* until its demise. The *New Statesman* created its own company, NS Distribution, which handled *New Society* until the two publications merged, and *City Limits*, the radical London listings magazine set up by former *Time Out* staff after an industrial dispute. *Time Out* has itself recently set up its own company, and *Tribune* has now taken on such a distributor.

But the principal effect of all this effort is only to slow the inherent decline to which, given the commercial logic of private enterprise distribution and the lack of resources for the sort of promotion campaigns larger publishers can mount, condemns the left press.

The free market does not guarantee free exchange of ideas; indeed, it positively hinders it.

The solution must lie in intervention which removes some of the commercial pressures on the distribution industry. For some, state intervention in publication and distribution would be the very definition of censorship. But I have sought to show that this definition is a distortion of the facts. For the state to intervene to widen the range of available publications would be the opposite of censorship.

In France, the law requires equal access for all titles to the distribution network. The biggest commercial wholesaler, National Messageries due Presse Parisien, NMPP, is privately-owned by Hachette, the French equivalent of W.H. Smith, and a co-operative of all the publishers involved. The result is that a wider range of titles is available to French readers than to their British counterparts.

It seems likely that this distribution system has greatly helped the survival, for example, of *Libération*, the independent left daily, which is widely available through France, with a six-figure circulation

– a sharp contrast to the problems faced by Britain's left-wing periodicals which have difficulty in reaching a tenth of those numbers.

Such a system would not, of course, overcome the promotion problems faced by smaller publishers. The 1977 Royal Commission on the Press, though, recommended a fund to redistribute advertising revenue in a way which would help small-circulation titles. It made no recommendations about distribution; but revenue sharing coupled with easier distribution could transform the position of small periodicals, ease access for new titles, and open up the possibilities for a more varied periodical press.

Care would have to be taken that any such system was not seen as an imposition on the more marginal retailers. British readers would perhaps have to get used to paying more for their reading; French periodicals do cost more.

But we must ask: Does a country which claims to value the free exchange of ideas in print have the will to establish the means to make it a reality? Or is this lofty ideal simply a respectable cover for a commercial system which enables many to make profits – at the cost of real pluralism of opinion?

7 Academic Freedom at Risk

Sir Kenneth Alexander

> Where there is much desire to learn, there of necessity will be much arguing, much writing, many opinions: for opinion in good men is but knowledge in the making.
>
> John Milton, *Areopagitica*, 1644

Freedom of thought and freedom to publish are key elements in any democratic society. Academic freedom is a major element in these larger freedoms. In complex societies, where education employs a substantial proportion of the best educated people the encouragement or discouragement of critical thought, particularly amongst the young, exerts great influence on the democratic process, and thereby on every aspect of life and work.

There is a tendency to take this freedom for granted. In Britain 'academic freedom' is accepted as desirable and most academics assume that they can exercise this freedom in their teaching, research and writing. It is wise, however, to recognise that, like democracy itself, academic freedom is a tender plant. The twentieth century has seen powerful challenges to democracy, and academic freedom has always been a main target in these challenges. Listen to the Minister of Education in the Vichy government in wartime France: 'Among all the idols we must tear down, there is none we more urgently need to get rid of than this Descartes, whom people have wished to represent as the ultimate representative of French genius. He must be tossed out of the window'.[1] The various elements which together make a democracy extend beyond the governmental core of franchise, electoral process and Parliament to freedom of thought, worship, press and assembly; these democratic rights can be under threat even at times when the core appears to be at no risk. The practice of freedom – in the media, in academia, in voluntary organisations including political parties – is at least as important for freedom as this governmental core. There is evidence to suggest that when democracy is at risk it is these peripheral (but crucial) areas which first feel the pressure. For a number of reasons, reflected in a variety of forms, the 1980s in Britain have seen more open attempts to rein in the exercise of academic freedom than possibly in any other decade this century. From my own experience of 40 years as teacher and administrator in five universities I have no doubt that this has been true for the second half of the twentieth century.

Before turning to the evidence it is necessary to look more closely at the complexities of academic freedom in higher education. Freedom for whom and to do what? Most directly involved are the students and the academics. Emphasis is usually placed on the freedom exercised by the teachers and researchers, but students have distinctive interests such as barriers to entry, possibilities of involvement and influences on course structure and content, fairness in examining and the awarding of degrees; and the extent to which student affairs are governed by students or, alternatively, by university administrations. The interests of staff concern the extent to which departmental, faculty and institutional administration and policies can be influenced by them, their elected representatives and their trade union. Issues include the openness of and the criteria used in the appointing and promotion processes; the allocation of teaching and other duties; freedom to choose research topics; freedom to express views in lectures and to publish what may be regarded as unorthodox or even erroneous. Security of employment, tenure, as the guarantee of academic freedom has attracted much attention and is important, but even more important is the established atmosphere and practice of the institution, the extent to which freedom of thought and expression is valued and exercised.

This synopsis of the elements of academic freedom makes it clear that the enlargement of one person's freedom may place some constraint on the freedom of another. The proposal once advanced by a Prices and Incomes Board that teaching ability should be rewarded on the basis of student assessment was rejected by academics as a threat to academic freedom. The allocation of resources – finance for research, lecture loadings etc. – will enhance the academic freedom of some at the expense of others. Just as effective democracy must take account of different, and to some extent conflicting, interests, academic freedom must take account of the different objectives and values of the members of an academic community.

It is tempting but too easy to propound and defend absolute principles and governing rules for freedom within universities, but to do so overlooks the conflicts of interest which have to be accommodated. Any freedom which rests on the use of resources must be relative freedom. Even freedom of thought, expression and dissemination must take account of the perceived interests of some restraining the freedom of others. When students claim that some lectures are 'a waste of time' or 'confusing', or when one academic protests that a colleague is teaching 'nonsense' which undermines his or her ability to instil 'sense' into students, issues of academic freedom are raised and there is no resolution which can leave all parties satisfied. We can agree with Burke that abstract liberty, like other mere abstractions, is not to be found, but the qualifications to freedom which must arise when conflicting values, interests and objectives exist should not be allowed to cloud the importance of the most fundamental aspects of academic freedom, freedom of thought and expression.

In contemporary Britain universities are dependent on finance from government. This finance comes by three main routes: from the University Grants Committee, the Research Councils and in student fees (provided for UK students by central or local government). The UGC contribution is the most important in magnitude and because it meets the high overheads of running a university. The UGC is to be replaced by a Universities Funding Council which, like its predecessor, will be appointed by the Secretary of State for Education and Science in consultation with other ministers who have a departmental interest. (A newspaper has reported that a proposal to appoint one of Britain's most senior (in terms of responsibility) and successful industrial managers to the Funding Council has been dropped because his politics are not those of the Government.) The Education Reform Bill provided that the Council should comply with any directions given to it by the Secretary of State and that the sums distributed to the universities would be paid 'subject to such terms and conditions' as the Secretary of State determines. On this basis the Minister's powers would have been unlimited; and there was no provision for the Council to advise the Minister. Furthermore the Bill specified that universities could be required to repay the entire grant in the event of any breach, in any respect, of the terms and conditions laid down by the Funding Council. This proposal involves a major shift from the previous arrangement: 'the convention has been established that the Government do not enquire into, or question, the UGC's recommendations as to the allocation between the universities of the total amounts on which the Government has decided.'[2] It was this convention that allowed government, time and again in Parliament and elsewhere to deny responsibility for the distribution of funds between universities, and cushion itself against criticism of the cuts in grant.

Naturally the universities have been worried by the changes proposed in this Bill. In an attempt to allay these worries, and to muster support in Parliament, the Under Secretary at Education and Science, Mr Robert Jackson, MP placed an article in *The Times* in which he argued that the problem was a general one, 'the familiar paradox that while the *form* of the British constitution is authoritative, even totalitarian, its *practice* is highly pluralistic' and that 'all this, which has protected the universities from detailed intervention by government throughout the era of the UGC will continue to operate in the new era of its successor, the UFC.'[3] Mr Jackson seemed unaware that in the universities the clauses in the Bill on financial control and on tenure were seen as a determination by government to consolidate and strengthen trends already revealed in attitudes to the universities. Mr Jackson's own attitudes, expressed immediately before he was given responsibility for higher education, may be taken as an illustration: 'The apparatus and ethos of the self-regarding academic producer-monopoly must be dismantled.'[4]

The heavy dependence on government finance presents a continuing threat to the autonomy of British universities. If the value of this autonomy is accepted as desirable in the interests of freedom of thought and freedom to initiate, then tightening the control element which stems from this dependence, as proposed in the Bill, would be a dangerous move in the wrong direction. After much criticism in Parliament and in the country, and amendments carried in the Lords, the proposed tightening of control was modified. The risk to academic freedom remains large, however, as long as the universities remain so dependent on government finance. It was perfectly fair of Mr Jackson to describe the university system as an 'academic producer-monopoly'; it is the form and substance of government influence over finance and student quotas which have made it so. The lurking threats to academic freedom would be more easily resisted if government direct grant (through the Funding Council) were reduced and the level of fees paid by students increased. Government authority over the universities would be reduced and the student consumer would be in a much stronger position to influence university policy. But there are obvious dangers. The financial enfranchisement of students must not be at the expense of expanding educational opportunity for those from families with relatively low incomes. At a time when the demographic trend creates opportunities for widening educational opportunity, the introduction of a loan system insensitive to this objective would almost certainly reduce the already very small representation of social groups C and D in our universities. To waste the present opportunity to correct this social imbalance in the interests of reducing the risks to academic freedom of the present high dependency on direct government funding would be too high a price to pay. Nevertheless the possibilities of constructing a new approach to funding which improves freedom and expands access deserves exploration.

Another issue raised by the Education Reform Bill and which affects academic freedom is tenure. There is no U-turn on the intention 'to give the universities and other institutions to which the provisions apply the possibility of accommodating themselves to the changed economic circumstances by declaring staff redundant.'[5] Dismissals would be subject to safeguards; Commissioners would be appointed with the power to modify university statutes and establish an appeals procedure; staff declared redundant can also go to the Industrial Appeals Tribunal, machinery available to all employees. The House of Lords passed a minor but useful amendment which restricts redundancy to cases in which a university abolishes the post, thus protecting the established academic from being displaced and then replaced by another. Pressures to further qualify the abolition of tenure by extending the injunction to the new University Commissioners 'to apply the principles of justice and fairness' to include some explicit reference to academic freedom were resisted by the Lord Chancellor, arguing that a form of words properly reflecting the concept could not be worked out. Lord Blake suggested that it was as difficult to define 'fairness' and 'justice'. Lord Flowers, accepting that tenure was 'an outmoded privilege', emphasised 'the essential right of an academic to propose and test, by exposition and experiment within the law, unorthodox or unpopular views, without fear of dismissal on that score or of direct and narrow political harassment' and claimed that such academic freedom 'is of the essence of higher education and research'. Lord Jenkins of Hillhead, in a successful amendment, but with the Lord Chancellor arguing that it was difficult to legislate for abstract concepts, produced a definition: 'that academic staff have freedom within the law to question and test received wisdom and put forward new ideas and controversial or unpopular opinions, without placing themselves in jeopardy of losing their jobs or privileges they may have at their institutions.'

The Lord Chancellor's efforts to convince his fellow peers that academic freedom is not at risk faced the same difficulty as had Mr Robert Jackson, but without having contributed to the difficulty himself. When Lord Mackay argued that 'the Government is firmly committed to the cause of academic freedom' his sincerity was not doubted, but aspects of the Bill and statements by Ministers had sown a distrust within the universities and amongst those who shared their attachment to academic freedom. Shortly before the Lord Chancellor sought to 'heal the breach and assure universities that I and Ministers collectively in government appreciate academic freedom', the Prime Minister was reported as saying 'The rules of a civilised society are politeness and good-neighbourliness . . . This business of breaking the rules began in universities, where most of these theoretical philosophies always start. They never start with ordinary people.'[6] Such illiberal absurdity at the top is buttressed by a good measure of hostility at lower levels of government. Mr Jackson's speech at a London conference was described by Owen Surridge as viewing academics as people who should stop cowering in the secret garden of knowledge and get to grips with the real world since knowledge for its own sake was no longer the prime concern. (*Times Higher Education Supplement* 17.6.88.) This was quoted in the House of Lords at the time.[7] In this atmosphere it is not surprising therefore that the Lords were not to be satisfied with assurances and voted for a specific defence of freedom to be added to the Bill.

As well as debates about the general principles there have been specific issues raised by Ministers affecting academic freedom and seen as threatening it. Mr Keith Joseph (now Lord Joseph) saw it as his duty as Secretary of State for Education and Science to set up an investigation into the academic integrity of an Institute of Industrial Relations at the University of Warwick, with the result that three distinguished academics rejected the charge of bias which had been levelled at the Institute. In another instance the Department commissioned an investigation into two units, 'The Economy: A Social Process' offered by the Open University, in response to 'about half-a-dozen' written complaints and 'an unspecified number' of oral complaints, many of them made directly to the Secretary of State himself. The Vice-Chancellor was asked to review the course and 'if appropriate, to amend, withdraw or replace the course materials.' In open examination and discussion (the commissioned report was conducted in secret by unnamed economists) the charge of serious bias did not stand up, and the University stood its ground. The Minister also invited parents who were concerned that school teachers might be indoctrinating their children through an emphasis on peace in their teaching of international relations to send him their evidence. This campaign against peace studies has had considerable support in the media and from some academics. Dr Roger Scruton praises the Government 'for questioning much that passes for higher education in this country. When the tide of drivel has swollen to such proportion that the University of Bradford can offer a first degree in a subject ('Peace Studies') that doesn't even exist, it is surely time to ask whether there might not be better uses for the taxpayer's money'.[8] One wonders whether Dr Scruton is aware of both Defence Studies and War Studies as subjects established in British universities? It is reasonable to have reservations about the suitability for the first degree work of subjects focused on fairly narrow issues, but why the selectivity? It is incidents such as these and attitudes of this sort which are at the root of the fears for academic freedom at the present time, and these fears are being aroused by a government of the Right. Not that the Left is without fault in matters affecting academic freedom. In recent times there has been student action aimed at preventing freedom of speech, freedom to lecture (at Ruskin College) and freedom to attend lectures and sit examinations – each of these is a serious breach of academic freedom.

The test of genuine belief in freedom is its even-handedness. If, with Byron, we 'wish men to be free, as much from mobs as kings – from you as me' we must be prepared to defend the right to promote ideas we disagree with equally with the ideas we agree with. I believe that the vast majority of academics endorse such even-handedness. It seems more difficult for some politicians. Their own bias lends them to threaten the freedom of others who do not share it. The charge of bias against a university teacher or researcher is to some extent based on a misplaced belief in value-free opinion and theory. David Hume's insistence that reason must be the slave of passion was based on the recognition that objective reasoning plus absolute neutrality on values could only be barren. In my experience university teachers are fully aware of their responsibility to present alternative views for critical examination by students. Reading lists are the most obvious reflection of this. It is desirable that in subjects in which values play a part, and in which different theories compete, that departments should reflect these difficulties in their teaching and as far as possible in their staffing and recruitment policies. It is undesirable to expect good teachers to suppress their own strongly held views. Ideally problems of bias are more effectively dealt with by institutional balance than by attempts to curtail the freedom of individual teachers.

Given the tendency for issues of academic freedom to surface in social sciences it is worth noting that frequently the physical or natural sciences produce examples of established science resisting new ideas. In all academic disciplines we need academic freedom to shake firm faiths, for some such are barriers to human progress.

Some students, often the most active in politics on the left and on the right see even-handed impartiality as indifference and this had led to serious breaches of academic freedom. The 1986 Education (No. 2) Act designed to protect campus freedom has had some effect, but it is difficult to judge how it would operate if there were a return to the issues and the enthusiasms of the 1960s. (It is interesting to note, in the passing, that the drafters of this Act overcame the difficulties of legislating in favour of an abstract idea!) It is the responsibility of academic institutions to translate their concern for academic freedom into the promotion of academic qualities of respect for the opinions of others, and if respect is too much to ask for in some cases, at least an acceptance of the right to propagate views in circumstances where these can be examined critically and without rancour.

The Ruskin episode is still *sub-judice*. The Report of the Inspectors appointed by the Government, chaired by Sir Albert Sloman, could be taken as a manifesto for academic freedom in the future. The Education Committee and the Governing Council of the College have seen it as such and produced a statement of the principle of academic freedom (27 October 1987) which is much more detailed than exists in most universities. It is interesting to note that the Sloman Report recognises that in the protection of the rights of staff Ruskin's Terms and Conditions of Service is more comprehensive and explicit than comparable provision in universities.

On the abolition of tenure the Government has made much of the fact that only about half of British universities give contracts including tenure to their academic staff. What is the threat to academic freedom if 50 per cent of our universities are indistinguishable in terms of freedom from the other 50 per cent? It is important to understand that all universities have behaved as if their academic staff had tenure, and that most staff have assumed that they had tenure. Now that a duty to protect academic freedom has been placed upon the new University Commissioners I doubt if things will be very different in the short run. The issues are complex and the strength of the safeguards have yet to be tested. It is as well to recognise that with tenure gone the risks are increased that mavericks will find themselves over-represented amongst the redundant, and that this must be resisted.

Tenure has given protection to scholars whose work has been contained in a very narrow field, with little or no market demand for the knowledge and skill involved outside the university system. If a university decides, either for academic reasons or in response to financial cuts, to curtail or bring to an end its interest in such a subject specialisation there may be no appropriate alternative employment. Such specialists are essential if the frontiers of knowledge are to be extended, and their numbers will diminish unless their particular form of job insecurity is otherwise rewarded.

This issue relates to research. The dual funding of research by government in part through the UGC and in part through the Research Councils has been regarded as a great strength, enabling research initiatives to be taken which would face greater difficulties in a more centralist system. Recent statements by a one-time chairman of the Science and Engineering Research Council indicate the strength of government influence on the use of research funds. Sir John Kingman has referred to frequent instructions which if not complied with would have breached the Act or produced a formal direction from the Minister. There was continual interference in both major and minor matters, backed by the threat of formal direction. In another sensitive area, social research, the commissioning Department of Health and Social Security has introduced a new contract giving it power to prevent publication. Academic freedom can be attacked from several quite different angles – denying financial support, blocking access to data, and restricting publication being three.

On the wider research front it is the Government's intention that a greater proportion of research activity should be directed at the new and emerging technologies which will increase economic and social wealth creation. Whereas in 1985 about 70 per cent of UGC funded research was basic or 'pure', that percentage could fall to somewhere between 20 and 30 per cent. The concern must be that because funding for research in Britain is low compared with most major competitors the absolute volume of basic research will suffer major cut-backs. Decision takers on research funding will have the difficult task of judging not only the likelihood of the research being success-ful but the probability of its successful exploitation in the market place. The judgemental qualities required, backed by scientific excellence and business experience, are very scarce. It is a common-place that 'picking winners' in new product terms is extremely difficult. The problem of picking applied research projects with strategic significance will be even more difficult.

The theoretical attractions of this new strategy should not be allowed to deny support to scientists who have a track-record of success even if the immediate value and use of their results is not clear. Much previous scientific endeavour now applied to meet human needs had no such mission, but was stimulated by curiosity and the desire to demonstrate originality and creativity. While the very high cost of most fundamental research must limit society's response to scientists' right to choose their own research topics, some scientists, not usually difficult to identify, will repay being given this academic freedom. The changes in science policy and funding threatened this aspect of academic freedom. 'But let the creative bird be caught in the net of the fowler, and duly caged – all experience goes to show that it rarely sings.'

The 1980s have seen a major effort made to change the structure and style of management in British universities. *The Jarratt Report* of March 1985 laid down the broad principles – more forward planning (yet with government finance announced year by year, and sometimes after the relevant financial year has begun!), more concentration of decision taking in the Council (Court in Scotland) on which academics are in a minority, and greater responsibility to and accountability from heads of departments. Sir Alex Jarratt is right to argue that 'one of the biggest risks to academic freedom lies in universities being incapable of marshalling their own resources to meet their own defined objectives', and he is both factual and sincere when he says that his committee were 'as careful as possible to avoid forcing universities into a management dominated system because it would not work.'[9] A major threat to academic freedom can arise when successive cuts, underfunding and possibly a looming deficit push the management of a university to pursue esssential economics, overriding elements in its democratic structure in the process. One result of underfunding has been the narrowing range of disciplines which a university can offer its students as the rationalisation process develops. The breadth of subjects available within a first degree defines the most liberating intellectual experience which a university can offer, especially if the inter-relationships between subjects can be developed and the seeds of a tree of knowledge are sown. Paradoxically it has been argued that over-specialisation has developed in part as a defence mechanism against encroachments by other disciplines on the academic freedom of particular specialisms.[10] What we may call 'intellectual autonomy' has had the effect of placing some teaching and much research into made-to-measure strait jackets.

The opportunities for breadth linked with cognitive unity have been considerably curtailed in Britain in the 1980s. The unfortunate convergence of severe financial cut-backs and the Government's view that higher education is part of an educational obstruction in the way of improved economic performance, and that this is based on an antipathy to enterprise, technology and even success itself leaves less and less room for breadth. The conflict between cognitive unity as an educational objective and the greater emphasis on relevance is obvious. As an economist who sees problem solving as a main activity I favour the switch to relevance but reject the false distinction which categorises philosophy, ethics, literature and history as irrelevant. It was encouraging to hear Keith Joseph make this point in a debate on the Education Reform Bill. Economic and commercial success are the foundations on which civilised living can be built, but other necessary conditions would include individual development derived from educational breadth.

The threats to academic freedom appear to be based in part on the Governments' suspicion that the hearts and minds of both students and academics are not wholly in tune with the values and objectives of 'the enterprise society', and in part arise as an unintended consequences of finance led cuts which have limited the scope for academic initiative. There is a measure of *naïveté* in the resentment which many British academics feel when their dependence on finance from government results in unwanted forms of surveillance and interference. The comfortable notion that the UGC was independent of government wore very thin in the early 1980s. There is greater realism now about what may and may not be expected from the new Funding Council. This realism should induce a greater vigilance, earlier sightings and greater readiness to counter-attack threats to academic freedom, in whatever form and from whatever source. There is disagreement within and beyond the walls of academia as to what should be the characteristics of the new Jerusalem, but whatever these are let academics resolve that they 'shall not cease from mental fight'.

Notes

1. Barrows Dunham, *The Heretics*, Eyre & Spottiswoode, London, 1963, page 325.
2. Special Report from the Committee of Public Accounts: *Parliament and Control of University Expenditure*. Session 1966–67 (H.C. Paper 290, pp. 246–7).

3.   *The Times*, 23 January 1988.

4.   *Times Literary Supplement*, 8 May 1987.

5.   *House of Lords Official Report*, Volume 497, No. 130, 19 May 1988, Column 485.

6.   *Scotsman*, 2 May 1988.

7.   Later, in a letter to the *Times Higher Educational Supplement*, Mr Jackson repudiated using these actual words and argued that this summary 'telescoped his argument'. However, he also added: 'I then went on to argue that the Government's emphasis on the diversification of funding away from overwhelming reliance on provision by the state should be seen as a positive strategy to promote a richer and more densely-textured interaction between higher education and society.'!

8.   *The Times*, 11 June 1985.

9.   A. Jarratt, 'The Management of Universities', *Journal of the Royal Society of Arts*, October 1986.

10.   Frederick Turner, 'Design for a New Academy', *Harper's Magazine*, N.Y., 1985.

8 The Right to Know
Maurice Frankel

In 1985 the MORI polling organisation asked people which two or three institutions they thought best protected their rights. Most nominated the police, followed someway down by the courts, trade unions and local councils. But the striking finding was at the bottom of the list. Only two per cent of people regarded the cabinet as significantly defending their rights. In fact, more people had confidence in international bankers, the City and the Bank of England than in ministers. This was not a reflection on Mrs Thatcher and her colleagues in particular – though it is certainly nothing for them to be proud of – for MORI obtained similar results with this question in 1973.[1]

What it does suggest is that people see government as self-serving, rather than serving them. An overwhelming priority of all governments is the desire to be seen as more competent than their opponents, and this is reflected in the contents and timing of any official report or ministerial statement. Anything that might undermine a policy to which government is committed or expose ministers to embarrassing criticism is a candidate for suppression.

In this game of political oneupmanship ministers' control of information is an unrivalled advantage. Not surprisingly, they will not relinquish it. The present government, like the Labour administrations of the 1970s, has resisted pressure for a freedom of information (FOI) act. Their objections may be presented in constitutional terms, but the real reason is their fear that FOI would weaken the government's ability to conceal its mistakes or defend policies when the evidence shows they don't work.

Freedom of information is a much greater threat to certain styles of government than others. Open policy making, where the government avoids final commitment until it has explored the options, examined obstacles and developed workable solutions, may find openness not only feasible but helpful. The government can draw on a wider more informed debate before deciding. A policy seen to emerge in this way may have greater public acceptance. And the policy itself may be sounder because unworkable proposals can be identified and jettisoned before they are adopted and without loss of face.

But an inflexible government which hastily commits itself to unworkable proposals cannot afford openness. Policy designed to placate a special interest group, implement a dogma, or generate instant popularity does not easily tolerate scrutiny. It survives only if the lack of analysis, the failure to anticipate problems and the often disastrous consequences are concealed. To such a government, freedom of information is a perpetual liability, constantly exposing it to criticism it cannot answer.

All governments work in this way at least some of the time. None, whatever its political complexion, would find freedom of information particularly easy to live with: but the public will always be better off. That is why FOI is a basic constitutional reform, which should appeal to supporters of the present government as much as to its opponents. There is evidence that this is in fact the case. A MORI poll conducted for the Campaign of Freedom of Information in 1986 found no statistically significant difference in the level of support for an FOI Act between Conservative voters (69 per cent in favour), and those voting for Labour (67 per cent) or the Alliance (68 per cent).[2]

A Freedom of Information Act would put into law the presumption that the public has the right to official information unless the government can show that disclosure would be harmful for one of a number of specified reasons: breach of privacy, or the disclosure of genuine military or trade secrets, for example. Government claims on these scores could be challenged either in front of the courts or an independent ombudsman with power to order disclosure.

The ability of such an independent body to overrule a minister has provoked an objection to FOI on 'constitutional' grounds. The theory is that ministers are accountable to parliament, and can be forced to disclose any information to it. Freedom of information legislation would supposedly subvert parliament's role by transferring to the courts the power to dictate what ministers must disclose. Not political self-interest, but this elevated constitutional argument leads ministers to proclaim, as Lord Elton (then a Home Office Minister) did in 1985, that an FOI Act is 'unacceptable to us in principle'.[3] Or, in Mrs Thatcher's words: 'Ministers' accountability to Parliament would be reduced and Parliament itself diminished'.[4]

The reality is that there is precious little accountability in parliament. Because the opposition is by definition the minority, ministers are only held to account if the government's supporters insist on it. But many on the government backbenches live in hope of a ministerial post: they know what will happen to their chances if they too actively seek to expose government incompetence or deceit. In any case, backbenchers share their ministers' interests in boosting the government's prestige at the expense of the opposition. If exposing ministerial blunders or complacency means risking damaging the government – and weakening their own chances of re-election – it is unlikely to happen.

Too often ministers are genuinely held to account only when blatantly incompetent or caught in outright lies. Even here the evidence frequently comes from press reporting and insider leaks rather than successful parliamentary inquisition. On countless important issues ministers simply decline to provide parliament with information, and nothing more is heard of the matter.

The fact is that MPs have no more *right* to information than any ordinary citizen. Anyone who imagines that the system of Parliamentary Questions (PQs) confers such rights should study the voluminous restrictions on what may even be *asked* in a PQ. But these are minor irritations alongside the more simple truth revealed in the standard guide to parliamentary practice: 'an answer cannot be insisted upon, if the answer be refused by a Minister'.[5]

Charles Medawar of Social Audit has catalogued the varied ways in which ministers refuse to answer:

> Information requested may be described as being 'not available', 'not separately recorded', 'not centrally recorded' or 'not recorded in government statistics'. Many refusals are given on the grounds that an answer could be obtained 'only at disproportionate cost'. Otherwise, ministers may say it is not 'appropriate' or 'usual' or 'the policy' or 'in accordance with normal practice' to give the information required. And some information is denied because it is formally 'confidential' and even 'classified'.[6]

A common excuse for refusing information is that producing it would involve 'disproportionate cost'. In October 1987 Mrs Thatcher was asked about this:

> *Mr Tony Banks* asked the Prime Minister what is the sum above which an answer to a parliamentary question is considered to represent disproportionate cost.
> *The Prime Minister*: It is for Ministers to decide whether to decline to answer a question on grounds of disproportionate cost. Any question likely to cost more than £200 is referred to the responsible Minister before significant resources are committed.
> *Mr Tony Banks* asked the Prime Minister how many questions she

has refused to answer since 1979 on the grounds of disproportionate costs.
The Prime Minister: This information can be supplied only at
disproportionate cost.[7]

The generously inclined may find in this the long sought evidence that
the Prime Minister has a sense of humour. It is more significant as a
blunt reminder of MPs' limited powers: they can only invite, not
demand, answers.

An insight into the way the government ignores the cost factor
when expedient arose in May 1988 when a Conservative backbencher
asked the Prime Minister to list the government's achievements since
1979. Mrs Thatcher produced a reply stretching across eight pages of
Hansard, the equivalent of a 90 minute speech.[8] The cost of
producing this reply, she later acknowledged, had been £3,900.[9]

SECRECY IN PRACTICE

The basis of the government's case against FOI is, in Lord Elton's
words, that it offends against the principle that 'it is not for Ministers
to decide what information should be released'.[3] A few examples
show how this discretion is exercised.

In 1988 the government announced it would stop publishing figures
for the number of people living on supplementary benefit, a basic
indicator of poverty. Between 1972 and 1985 the numbers rose from
5.9 million to 9.4 million.[10]

In 1983 the government suppressed a report by the Department of
Energy's policy unit which concluded that there was a case for
devoting more resources to energy conservation. Instead, a report
which reached precisely the opposite case was published.

The published report said: 'it is difficult to find an economic
justification for direct government involvement in fuel choices made
by consumers'. But the original unpublished report found 'there are
significant and continuing national benefits to be gained from increased conservation investment'. The published document said
there must be 'a presupposition that there is no Public-Sector
Borrowing Requirement advantage in bringing forward conservation'. But the suppressed report had concluded that 'in the longer
term, increased conservation investment should reduce the call on
public funds for energy supply'.[11]

Insight into how government stage manages information was provided by a leak in 1987 from the Ministry of Agriculture, Fisheries and Food. The 'Restricted' document, entitled 'Register of Environmental Achievements' was described in its introduction as partly for internal reference and partly 'as ammunition against those who criticise the Ministry's environmental record'. Projects likely to reflect credit on the Ministry were earmarked for massive publicity. A project designed to 'demonstrate the extent of the Department's commitment' to countryside conservation, 'improve the image of the farming industry' and encourage practical conservation was destined for 'before, during and after publicity ... on a national and regional scale'.

But publicity for a £300 000 project on radioactivity in food was 'not desirable'. Investigations into pesticide poisoning of farm animals were 'confidential'. Publicity for action on chemically contaminated food was 'not desirable'. And MAFF did not want publicity for 'consideration of environmental aspects in the context of water privatisation'.[12]

Sometimes it is only the fact that the government can stop the public learning what it knows that allows an unjustified policy to be sustained. The leaking in March 1982 of a confidential letter by Sir Henry Yellowlees, then Chief Medical Officer at the Department of Health and Social Security, changed the whole basis of the debate on lead in petrol. The letter acknowledged what the government had constantly denied, that: 'there is a strong likelihood that lead in petrol is permanently reducing the IQ of many of our children' and that 'hundreds of thousands of children' were at risk.[13] The letter had been in existence for over a year before it was leaked, during which time the government was able to dismiss concerns about lead pollution as 'exaggerated' and 'emotive'.

More recently, the government was forced to drop its opposition to a ban on flammable foam filled furniture partly as a result of the leaking of a previously secret document. The government had proposed to phase out the foams, which burn to produce highly toxic fumes, over a three-year period. But they would have been replaced by an equally toxic alternative which merely took two minutes longer to ignite. In January 1988 a highly critical memorandum by the government purchasing agency, the Crown Suppliers, was leaked. The document pointed out that a substantially safer foam existed – and was used in furniture bought for ministers' offices. It described the government's proposals as 'window dressing' adding that they 'cannot be the correct approach if safety is the paramount consideration'.[14] The leak contributed to the growing pressure on the government, and within days the government scrapped its original proposals and announced a total ban on the dangerous foams. Immediately afterwards Lord Young, the Trade and Industry Secretary, ordered a leak inquiry to identify and punish the person responsible for the leak.[15] The government has always refused to identify those pesticides cleared for use in the UK with data from a US commercial laboratory now known to have carried out worthless and in some cases deliberately falsified safety studies. From American data is seemed likely that at least 18 pesticides which relied at least in part on this data were on sale in the UK in 1983.[16] The Ministry of Agriculture investigated but refused to disclose its findings. Several years after the problem was discovered (in the late 1970s) the Ministry announced that reliable alternative studies had finally been provided in all suspect cases. But it has refused to identify the pesticides implicated and failed to give warning of any kind to users of the suspect products.[17]

Studies on the safety of most food additives remain secret. Following enormous criticism, the Ministry of Agriculture agreed to make data public – though only for new additives approved after 1986 and not the hundred already in use. A copy of such safety data is lodged with the Lending Division of the British Library. But when Dr Erik Millstone of Sussex University tried to borrow data for a single study on a widely used food dye known as 'Red F.123' he was told it was not available on loan. He could have it only if he paid for photocopies – which came to a total of £90. He estimates that to obtain the full data on this one additive alone would cost him over £5000.

These examples have been deliberately chosen because they illustrate the extent to which secrecy is the norm even in relation to safety and environmental matters where no issue of national security remotely arises. A similar response can be found in relation to personal files held on individuals by government departments, hospitals, employers and other bodies. Although people can see their own computer records under the Data Protection Act, 1984, the government has with minor exceptions resisted attempts to extend the right to non-computerised records. The Access to Personal Files Act 1987, the result of a private member's bill drafted by the Campaign for Freedom of Information and introduced by Archy Kirkwood MP was opposed by the government and allowed onto the statute books only after everything other than certain local authority records had been deleted.[18]

In June 1988 the government announced plans to reform the discredited Section 2 of the Official Secrets Act, which makes the unauthorised disclosure of any official information an offence. The most striking feature of the White Paper proposals is that they are not designed to reduce official secrecy at all. This is made clear in the White Paper itself:

> The White Paper ... does not ... address such matters as the question of public access to official information... That is a separate issue which does not arise directly out of the reform of Section 2.

The proposed reform, it says:

> does not mean ... that there will be no inhibition on the disclosure of any of the information which the criminal law will no longer protect... Ministers will continue to determine what information should be disclosed.[19]

Although information in many areas will be removed from the scope of the new law it will not become more easily accessible to the public. Anyone leaking it will face possible disciplinary action or dismissal. MPs will have no new power to demand information from ministers; the public no new right to information on pollution, dangerous products, government files held on them or the impact of new policies on their communities.

In many ways, the new law will retain the worst aspects of the old Section 2 in a more concentrated form.[20] Disclosures of *any* information in certain areas will be an absolute offence: harm will not have to be proved, and no defence will exist for a civil servant or journalist charged. In other areas, where a test of harm is proposed, no public interest defence will be permitted. A person disclosing information in order to expose fraud, negligence, massive incompetence or reckless disregard for public safety will not be able to plead justification.

A Freedom of Information Act is no longer a utopian vision. Nine countries already have such legislation including Australia, Canada and New Zealand, countries with parliamentary systems closely resembling ours; as well as the USA, France, Norway, Sweden, Denmark and the Netherlands. Early in 1988 the Italian government announced its own plans for a FOI Act.

The basis of these laws is a general public right to all official information, with exceptions only for information falling into specifically exempted categories. The exemptions typically cover information harmful to (but not *all* information *about*) national security, foreign relations or law enforcement, personal privacy, corporate trade secrecy and so on. The advice of individual civil servants is typically exempted also, though not expert technical opinion. Although these categories are wide, government claims for secrecy can be tested in the courts or by appeal to an independent ombudsman. The government must be able to show in refusing a request that it is for reasons more substantial than embarrassment to a minister or inconvenience to a department.

The legislation has proved enormously popular. In 1984 the eight largest US federal agencies received a total of a quarter of a million FOI requests. Some 47 000 requests were made under the Canadian Act in 1986–87, the majority for personal files. In Australia, 36 500 requests were made in 1985–86.

Disclosures under the US FOI Act include:

1. A Louisville newspaper obtained federal inspection reports on nursing homes which showed that residents were being abused. As a result of the paper's campaign new state legislation to regulate such homes was introduced: many were closed down and several charged with fraud.

2. The Union of Concerned Scientists obtained raw data used in an official study which concluded that the chances of being injured in a nuclear accident were the same as being struck by a meteor. They showed the data did not support this conclusion. Following their re-analysis the Nuclear Regulatory Commission agreed that the study was faulty and withdrew its previous endorsement of it.

3. The Health Research Group revealed that excessive radiation was being produced by X-ray machines at breast cancer screening centres. In some cases levels were 25–30 times too high. Within months of the disclosure all centres involved had significantly cut emissions.

4. Disclosures of tax audit reports showed that eight per cent of individuals whose tax returns had been audited had paid too much tax and were owed refunds.

5. The State of New Mexico used the FOI Act to show that the federal government's nuclear waste disposal programme in the state breached environmental regulations. It used the documents to bring legal action against the federal government for non-compliance.

6. Sir Freddy Laker used the Act to obtain transcripts of official meetings which revealed that US and UK governments and

airlines had conspired to exclude the Laker Skytrain from flying to the US. The exposure helped Laker win the right to establish his new service.

7. Disclosures under the Act revealed disastrously lax security measures at nuclear power plants. Documents released in 1976 showed there had been ten arson attacks, three unexplained break-ins and two bombs found at nuclear plants in previous years.

8. The Act has been used to provide consumer guides to the safety and effectiveness of drugs, the fees charged by doctors, and unpublished tax rulings made by the Inland Revenue Service.[21]

Sometimes FOI has prevented waste on a massive scale. A recent disclosure under the Australian Act forced the government to cancel a £266 million project to establish a new tank training area for the army. The documents showed that while the military were insisting on the purchase of a 2.5 million hectare site in New South Wales, an internal analysis had revealed that the site was wholly inadequate for its purpose. It was too mountainous for an effective firing range; it was covered by fog for 100 days of a year making it impossible to observe the results of target practice; and the weather was too cold to simulate the tropical combat conditions in which the army expected to have to fight in a real conflict.

This episode suggests that there is little to the argument that FOI is an expensive burden. The savings resulting from the cancellation of this one project in Australia amounted to nearly 40 times the annual cost of the Australian Freedom of Information Act (around £6.9 million in 1985–86). Canada's Act is similarly inexpensive – the 1986–87 cost was around £5.6 million. For comparison, the amount spent annually by the UK's Central Office of Information on government publicity is currently more than £150 million a year.

Moreover, Australian government departments report that the Act has brought considerable benefits. Reporting on the departments' views of the Act after its first two years, the Australian Attorney General[22] described the views of the Department of Social Security:

... access ... has served to lessen mistrust and dissatisfaction with ... and improved the quality of decision making ... greater public access to the rules and guidelines used in making decisions ... has made those decisions more readily understood by the people affected. Departmental Officers are being urged to refer clients to the relevant manuals and guidelines when explaining decisions ...

clients who are adversely affected by a decision [have been able] to see the full facts of the decision before deciding to seek a review. In some areas this has reduced the numbers of appeals. In others it has assisted clients to better prepare and present appeals and thereby has expedited the review process.

Officers, particularly in client contact areas, have commented that the knowledge that the documentation of their work may be scrutinised by the person concerned has encouraged them to be more precise in documenting their work.

The Department of Industry and Commerce:

> ... saw improved decision making by officers with the knowledge that access to their decisions may be granted... Some bad decisions have been disclosed through FOI requests and subsequent remedial steps taken.

Other departments described: 'an improvement of record-keeping standards', 'increased community understanding of the [agency's] workings', 'a re-examination and streamlining of procedures', 'more consistent policy application', the 'resolving [of] grievances that might otherwise have led to time consuming correspondence' and, in a comment which hints at former chaos, the reorganisation of files so that 'documents relating to a subject are now consolidated and staff can determine why certain actions are taken'.

What are the prospects for FOI in Britain? There is no sign that Mrs Thatcher has modified the views she gave in a 1979 parliamentary answer:[23]

> *Mrs Renée Short* asked the Prime Minister whether she intends to bring forward legislation to establish a public right of access to official information.
> *The Prime Minister*: No.
> *Mrs Renée Short* asked the Prime Minister if she is satisfied with the current public right of access to official information.
> *The Prime Minister*: Yes.

However, in other countries FOI laws have been introduced by Conservative governments. Progress conceivably might be made under a Conservative government in Britain led by a different Prime Minister. Even the present government has been unable to resist the recent stream of Private Member's Bills on FOI issues. Backbench Bills which have reached the statute books – often against initial government opposition – include the Local Government (Access to Information) Act 1985, the Access to Personal Files Act 1987, the Access to Medical Reports Act 1988, the Environment and Safety Information Act 1988, the Community Health Councils (Access to Information) Act 1988, and (opening the land registry to inspection) the Land Registration Act 1988.

At the 1987 general election the Labour and Alliance party manifestos all contained pledges to introduce a Freedom of Information Act. The attractions of FOI to an opposition party – whose work is constantly frustrated by secrecy – may diminish when in office. Although Labour's October 1974 manifesto contained a promise to introduce FOI, the opportunity was never taken. It should not however be assumed that this pattern will necessarily be repeated. The Labour Party's most senior figures of the early 1970s never professed a commitment to FOI. This is no longer the case, and all opposition leaders in recent years have made repeated personal commitments.

It is however worth recalling the comment of a senior figure in the Australian Labour Party on his party's promise to strengthen the Australian FOI Act (which had been passed by a Conservative government) if elected. 'If we're going to legislate on FOI', he said, 'we will have to do it in our first year in office – before we have any secrets of our own to hide'.

Notes

1. Survey based on interviews with 1971 adults carried out in April 1985. *The Times*, 1.7.85.
2. Market & Opinion Research International Limited, 'Public Attitudes Towards Freedom of Information in Britain', July 1986. Research Study conducted for the Campaign for Freedom of Information, based on interviews with 1909 members of the general public.
3. *Hansard*, Lords, 19.3.85.
4. Letter to the Campaign for Freedom of Information, 1983. Quoted in: Wilson, D. *The Secrets File. The Case For Freedom of Information in Britain Today*, Heinemann Educational Books, London, 1984.
5. Erskine May, *Parliamentary Practice. The Law, Privileges, Proceedings and Usage of Parliament*, 20th edition, p. 342.
6. Medawar, C. *Parliamentary Questions – and Answers*, Social Audit, London 1980.
7. *Hansard*, Commons, 29 October 1987, columns 358–9.

8.   *Hansard*, Commons, 6 May 1988, columns 628–643.
9.   *Hansard*, Commons, 12 May 1988, column 195.
10.   *Daily Telegraph*, 13 July 1988.
11.   *Guardian*, 3 March 1983.
12.   Campaign for Freedom of Information, *Secrets* newspaper, No. 12, April 1987.
13.   Wilson, D. *Pressure: The A to Z of Campaigning in Britain*, Heinemann, London, 1984.
14.   *Guardian*, 8 January 1988.
15.   *Guardian*, 15 January 1988.
16.   Frankel, M. 'Pesticide Scandal', Friends of the Earth Newspaper, Autumn 1983.
17.   Frankel, M. 'How Secrecy Protects the Polluter' in Wilson, D. *The Secrets File*, Heinemann, London, 1984.
18.   The final Act deals only with housing and social work records though the government also undertook to make equivalent regulations on access to education records using existing powers at the same time. See: Campaign for Freedom of Information *Secrets* newspapers No. 12, April 1987 and No. 13, October 1987.
19.   Reform of Section 2 of the Official Secrets Act 1911, Cmnd 408, HMSO, June 1988.
20.   Campaign for Freedom of Information, Comment on the White Paper: Reform of Section 2 of the Official Secrets Act 1911, 8 July 1988.
21.   Hendricks, E. *Former Secrets. Government Records Made Public Through the Freedom of Information Act*, Campaign for Political Rights, Washington DC, 1982.
22.   Freedom of Information Act 1982, Annual Report by the Attorney General on the Operation of the Act 1983–84. Australian Government Publishing Service, Canberra, 1985.
23.   *Hansard*, Commons, 4 December 1979, column 93.

9 The Secrecy Act or the Public Interest?

Richard Shepherd

Two principal arguments informed the quest for reform of Section 2 of the Official Secrets Act 1911.

First, the present section, by protecting the unauthorised disclosure of all official information with penal sanctions, was both an affront to democratic principles of accountability and an increasingly ineffective defence of that category of information the unauthorised release of which could cause a real and serious injury to our national interest.

The second argument is that the ability of the citizen to argue detailed fact will lead to better informed discussion of public policy and in turn to greater accountability and possibly more successful decision taking. The post-1979 corollary is to be seen in the economic vitality achieved by central government's ordered retreat from the detailed management of major industries and of the economy in general. The corporatist view of Britain which had nurtured and sustained what appeared to be inexorable national economic decline was dependent on the presentation of an increasingly counterproductive stranglehold on the economic levers.

Covert cross-subsidy, grand central planning with corporatist barons bent on the sisyphean task of reordering the market place, linked to bureaucratic and ministerial instincts for secrecy – or the fear of testing the often limited intellectual basis for policy against the wider reaches of informed opinion – made for an easier execution of policy even if it was not always either a satisfactory or even effective policy in terms of what may have been too ill-considered objectives. Widening the circle of informed discussion may not always produce better policy but it will produce a clearer understanding of objectives and, possibly, pitfalls. It may also expose incompetence and complacency. But certainly it will lead to a better understanding of policy issues and political responses. To be gainsaid by argument and reason is more compatible with consent in a democracy than to be driven by narrow prejudice directed by a small circle of ministers supported by a limited concept of mandate. I would argue that the widening of responsibility in the economic field since 1979 and the recognition of the market has been one of the single great achievements of the Government and one that broke with the post-war corporatist consensus. And it has served our interests well.

Section 2 has long been recognised as not only ineffective but also counterproductive. It has nurtured instincts that have inhibited serious discussion of areas of public policy and it has had an insidious and limiting effect on the press coverage of sensitive political and social issues; issues incidentally that are considered legitimate matters of public debate in those nations to which we are inextricably bound by the nature of our common democracies. One only has to contrast serious press coverage of public policy in the United States or Canada with that in Britain. There seems to be here a greater cosying up to executive government and a preoccupation with transmitting the often unchallenged nostrums of ministers as if that were the central purpose of a free press. The Parliamentary Press Gallery has too often been employed as a Hallelujah Chorus for untested propositions and Whitehall seems too preoccupied with the management of the release of information than with the development of argued policy.

In his evidence to the Franks Committee, Professor Wade, then Professor of English Law, submitted that:

> The law as it now stands shows a complete failure to understand that accessibility of information about the government of the country is of vital importance in a democracy. It is so crude, and so excessively severe, that it is rendered tolerable in practice only by the Attorney General's tight control of prosecutions. It has the insidious effect of conditioning ministers and civil servants to believe that unauthorised disclosure of any official information ought to be a crime... It lowers the reputation of the public service, since it is thought to be used for covering up mistakes, even when this is not true. It has aggravated the secretiveness for which British administration has a bad name with its best informed critics, from the Fulton Committee to Mr Crossman. It has become one of the great vested interests of government. It is a classic example of bad law creating bad practice.
>
> (Departmental Committee on Section 2 of the Official Secrets Act 1911 (Chairman Lord Franks) Cmnd 5104 1972 Volume 2, pp. 411–12)

It is understandable that anyone exercising authority may not be too keen to have to explain the true reasons for decisions or to submit to detailed, critical examination of them. This may expose the extent to which instinct, guess work, deference to poor precedent or prejudice effect important policy initiatives. An informed discussion may even reveal the extent to which mistakes are made. Repealing Section 2 and replacing it with a more narrowly targeted range of protected information will not of itself shake off the instinct of secrecy nurtured by a culture reflecting the spirit of Section 2.

Other democratic nations, even those with similar institutions, have approached this problem by identifying a general public right to official information, often through a Freedom of Information Act, and strictly limiting the exemptions to this general presumption. Perhaps due to what Bagehot identified as the deferential nature of British society this is a surprisingly difficult argument to promote within our particular national context. There seems to be an instinctive nervousness about the consequences of enlarging informed argument and the objections adduced range very wide indeed. There seems to be a general, often unstated, fear that disclosure of information will make the business of government 'more difficult'. The arguments against a public right of general access to information are often unstated and rely on an unexamined prejudice that broadly the existing arrangements are not unreasonable and work fairly well. I do not accept this and would hold as testimony the post-war experience. Better informed debate will encourage the vitality of ideas and policy necessary to the regeneration of our national spirit and effectiveness.

At an early stage of preparation for the Private Member's Bill I was to introduce it was decided that the focus for reform should be Section 2 of the Official Secrets Act, 1911 and not a wider Freedom of Information measure. The judgement was formed by the belief that a narrowly targeted reform of Section 2 was more likely to be acceptable to Parliament and that there was a wider consensus of agreement on this issue across the floor of the House than on Freedom of Information legislation. This was obviously a disappointment to Professor James Cornford, Maurice Frankel, Des Wilson and the Campaign for the Freedom of Information, both on the grounds that it was not tackling the wider and more important issue of the wider rights of citizens to access to official information that affects every area of our national life and has a direct bearing on the citizen. Notwithstanding their disappointment, the Campaign generously offered to contribute their resources and abilities to the preparation of a draft bill. So too did Jonathan Aitken, the quite exceptional

Member of Parliament for Thanet South, who had in 1971 as a working journalist been prosecuted and acquitted under Section 2 along with Colonel Douglas Cairns, a former member of the international team of Military Observers in Nigeria, and Mr Brian Roberts, the editor of the *Sunday Telegraph*. The charges in this action had related to an article published in the *Sunday Telegraph* which had quoted extracts from a British diplomat's report on the Nigerian Civil War. The revelations seemed to support the charge that the then Labour Government had been less than candid to Parliament about the level of British arms supplies to the Nigerian Government during their civil war against Biafra. In the event the defendants were acquitted on all counts and Mr Justice Caulfield directed that their costs should be paid out of public funds. In his summing up Mr Justice Caulfield suggested that Section 2 of the Official Secrets Act 'should be pensioned off' in the interests of free speech. The by then Prime Minister, Mr Edward Heath, set up a committee of enquiry into the Official Secrets Act under the chairmanship of Lord Franks which reported in September 1972. The Franks Report has been the starting point for every mooted legislative reform since. It was the basis on which the Labour Government proposed to legislate, it was the basis of the 1979 Protection of Official Information Bill and it was the basis of my Private Member's Bill.

The Franks Report had provided the basis for widespread agreement on the need to replace Section 2 of the OSA and on the Committee's conclusion that the section was 'a mess'. Franks referred to the section's 'catch all quality', noting that

> It catches all official documents and information. It makes no distinctions of kind, and no distinctions of degree. All information which a Crown Servant learns in the course of his duty is 'official' for the purposes of Section 2, whatever its nature, whatever its importance, whatever its original source. A blanket is thrown over everything, nothing escapes.

The Franks Committee concluded that Section 2 suffered from so many defects that the only satisfactory approach was to repeal it and replace it by entirely new measures. The present Government attempted such a reform in 1979 but felt obliged to withdraw it after its Second Reading debate in the House of Lords when it had attracted some adverse comment on the concept of not permitting an independent review of a minister certifying that an offence had taken place. The curious history of prosecutions under the 1911 Act by governments of both parties ensured a certain anxiety that an unreviewable ministerial attestation that a serious injury had been caused was contrary to the spirit of a defendant's right to challenge a contention for which he might lose his liberty. These doubts about the 1979 Bill became an avalanche when Fleet Street realised that the Government's Bill would have prevented them from exposing the treachery of Anthony Blunt and the nature of the immunity from prosecution he had accepted nearly 20 years earlier.

By August 1987 eight years had passed since that abortive attempt and a succession of misplaced prosecutions, government embarrassment and backbench concern had convinced me and Parliamentary colleagues that there was both an opportunity and sufficient of a consensus in Parliament to replace Section 2 with a new bill. This would give more certain protection to that information which we agreed if released could cause 'serious injury' to our national interest, but would also release from the sanction of the criminal law all other information the release of which would not meet the serious injury test of the Franks Committee. The issues were thrashed out in meetings during August and September of the 1987 recess with Professor Cornford, Maurice Frankel and Jonathan Aitken. A former Parliamentary colleague and a passionate and effective campaigner for citizen's rights of access to official information, Steven Norris, also took part in these preliminary discussions. It was on the basis of these discussions and with the objective of more narrowly targeting the categories of information to be protected that I approached the Home Secretary, Douglas Hurd, in late September 1987. The sponsors included the former Home Secretary, Mr Merlyn Rees, who sat on the Franks Committee and who had been responsible in 1978 for the Labour Government's White Paper presaging reform, the former Foreign Secretary, Dr David Owen, and a former Lord Privy Seal with Foreign Office responsibilities, Sir Ian Gilmour, along with Jonathan Aitken, Sir Nicholas Bonsor, Sir Nicholas Fairbairn, Robin Squire, Teddy Taylor, Michael Foot, Chris Smith and Archy Kirkwood. All felt that the time was right for reform, that our proposals had integrity and that they made the case for a better balance to be drawn between the rights of citizens and the needs of government. In fact we were prepared to make the Bill available to government and provide the Parliamentary time that we had available through the Private Member's Bill procedure. We saw it as both proper and essential to seek the greatest possible

collaboration with the Government in reconciling the various contentions. Indeed this was regarded as of considerable importance by a
number of sponsors and also Parliamentary colleagues who in the
course of our canvassing responses to our draft Bill had expressed
support for reform. The draft Bill had a wide circulation in an
endeavour both to seek opinion and support. The final version
reflected this process of consultation. In early October 1987 the
Home Secretary indicated that although a little work had been done
by the Government on looking at Section 2, the Government was
not, and was unlikely to be, in a position to indicate its views on
reform before the mooted date of our Second Reading debate. What
was clear was that the Home Secretary regarded the matter as one
that went to the 'heart of government'.

After consultation with some of the sponsors, I took the view that
in the absence of Government proposals this was a wholly appropriate measure for a backbencher to place before the House of Commons, in that Section 2 is a measure that affects the relationship of
the citizen to the state and the House of Commons to the Executive.
Unfortunately this view was not one shared by the Prime Minister.
She wrote on 28 October stating she found it 'difficult to see how a
Private Member's motion could be the appropriate vehicle for
amending the law dealing with the security of the State.' On behalf of
the sponsors I wrote again in mid-November expressing our view that
surely it wasn't *who* introduced the measure that was important, but
rather the substance of what was proposed. I wrote that we took
some encouragement from the fact that neither the Prime Minister
nor any member of the Government had expressed major disagreement with any of the content of the Bill and that we had always hoped
that this would be an issue that would secure the Government's
support. I emphasised that nothing in the Bill encroached on Section
1 of the Official Secrets Act and also asked if she would meet with the
sponsors. This the Prime Minister declined to do, re-emphasising that
she still believed that a Private Member's Bill was not 'the right
vehicle for amending the law in this difficult and sensitive area'. It
now began to emerge that the Government proposed to indicate that
it would publish a White Paper and hopefully legislate at some future
date. This was widely seen as a move to head off support for our
Protection of Official Information Bill, due to have its Second Reading on Friday 15 January.

Some of the sponsors were puzzled by the position the Prime
Minister seemed to be adopting. After all, there was a respectable

case to be made saying it was in the Government's interest to encourage the widest possible discussion of the issues involved to ensure that any legislation that subsequently emerged would command the greatest possible consensus. The House of Commons would provide the very best forum for this discussion. It has always been evident that the Government could amend the Bill and if after reasoned debate it was determined to defeat the Bill it could always use its majority on Report and Third Reading. No criticisms nor observations had been made at any stage on any of the contents of the Bill. Then on Thursday 17 December, for the first time in the history of the Conservative Party, the Government imposed a three-line whip against a Private Member's measure. The imposition of a three-line whip was totally unexpected and indicated more forcibly than anything a change and hardening of attitude in government. It was particularly surprising in that no Conservative had opposed the Second Reading of Sir Clement Freud's 1978 Private Member's Bill on Freedom of Information which by definition had to deal with reform of Section 2, nor had the Home Secretary or Prime Minister identified any specific objection to any of the contentions contained in our Bill.

Nevertheless the Bill was opposed by the Government on a three-line whip and was consequently defeated by 271 votes to 234.

In its general outline our Bill followed the structure recommended by the Franks Report and adopted in the government's own 1979 Bill. Six protected categories of information, whose unauthorised disclosure would be an offence, were defined.

The first four were information about defence, international relations, security and intelligence whose unauthorised disclosure would be likely to cause 'serious injury' to the interests of the nation or endanger the safety of a citizen. In the Government's 1979 Bill the serious injury test had applied only to defence and international relations information. Our Bill adopted the Franks proposal that the test should apply to security and intelligence information as well.

The fifth category dealt with information likely to be useful in committing a crime, helping an escape from custody, or otherwise impeding law enforcement.

The sixth covered information provided by an individual to government in confidence in accordance with a statutory requirement (for example, the requirement to declare income to the Inland Revenue) or in connection with an application for a statutory benefit (such as legal aid or social security). The 1979 Bill had included two additional classes, which we regarded as redundant (though they appear once more in the Government's 1988 White Paper proposals for reform). All information about, or obtained from the interception of, communication was protected in the 1979 Bill. Under our Bill such disclosures would be caught only if they resulted in serious injury. In addition, the 1979 Bill protected all information supplied to the Government in confidence by foreign governments or international bodies. Again, our Bill would have caught such disclosures only where serious injury was involved.

The Bill contained a number of new defences.

REVIEW OF SERIOUS INJURY

The Franks Report, the Labour Government's 1978 Official Secrets White Paper, and the Conservative Government's 1979 Bill had all agreed that prosecutions involving a 'serious injury' test should rely on a conclusive ministerial certificate. Thus, in the 1979 Bill where the prosecution alleged that disclosures of defence or international relations information had caused serious injury, the injury would be proven by a certificate signed by the minister which the defence could not challenge.

We felt this was wholly unacceptable. However we doubted whether we would be able to convince Parliament that the issue should be left to a jury. The Bill therefore proposed an alternative form of review in which a ministerial certificate could be challenged in front of the Judicial Committee of the Privy Council – in effect, the Law Lords. Before a prosecution commenced they would hear evidence on whether such injury was actually likely. If they ruled that it was not, the prosecution could not proceed. The embarrassment to the government of having a case thrown out in this way would provide a substantial safeguard against the risk of ill-considered claims of serious injury.

PRIOR PUBLICATION

It would have been a defence to show that the information involved had already become publicly available, whether in the UK or elsewhere. This reflected a basic objective of the Bill that only disclosures likely to cause actual and serious harm should attract criminal penalties. A disclosure which merely repeats what is already published should not be an offence – for the harm will have been done by the original publication. Significantly, the 1979 Bill did allow a prior publication defence, but only in relation to information obtained from third parties or information about law enforcement. Our Bill would have provided the defence in relation to any protected information.

PUBLIC INTEREST

The Bill contained a public interest defence, defined as follows:

> It shall be a defence for a person charged with an offence under this Act to prove that the disclosure . . . of the information . . . was in the public interest insofar as he had reasonable cause to believe that it indicated the existence of crime, fraud, abuse of authority, neglect in the performance of official duty or other misconduct.

Where a civil servant (as opposed to a journalist or other person) was involved the defence would only have been available

> . . . if he has taken reasonable steps to comply with any established procedures for drawing such misconduct to the attention of the appropriate authorities without effect.

Such a defence would be available only where there is evidence of specific misconduct. It would not be open to a defendant to claim that a disclosure was justified because he or she maintained that the policy of the government itself (for example, membership of NATO) was against the public interest.

The types of misconduct that might arise would not be exhaustively defined. It would be open to a defendant to claim that such matters as, for example, a minister lying to Parliament, constituted misconduct.

However, it would not be sufficient for a defendant to show that some misconduct, however minor, had arisen. The misconduct must be sufficient to justify, in the public interest, the disclosure of information which ought normally to remain confidential.

Conclusive proof of the misconduct would not be required: in some cases it would be impossible to obtain such proof without an official inquiry or, in the case of an alleged crime or fraud, a trial. However, a person would not be justified in acting simply on suspicion. He or she would have to have 'reasonable cause to believe' that the information indicates the existence of misconduct; this implies that any reasonable person faced with similar information would reach the same conclusion.

This defence is analogous to the 'public interest' or 'iniquity' defence which exists in relation to actions for breach of confidence under common law. The defence evolved from rulings in the last century where the courts refused to enforce the normal obligation of confidentiality where to do so would help someone suppress evidence of his own wrongdoing. In the 1865 case of *Gartside* v. *Outram* the judge ruled:

> The true doctrine is, that there is no confidence as to the disclosure of iniquity. You cannot make me the confidant of a crime or fraud, and be entitled to close up my lips upon any secret which you have the audacity to disclose to me relating to any fraudulent intention on your part; such a confidence cannot exist. ([1856], 26 LJ Ch. 113, 114)

In subsequent rulings the courts have held that the defence is not restricted to the exposure of crime or fraud. In a 1968 case Lord Denning ruled that the defence

> extends to any misconduct of such a nature that it ought in the public interest to be disclosed to others ... [It] should extend to crimes, frauds *and misdeeds* [emphasis added], both those actually committed as well as those in contemplation, provided always – and this is essential – that the disclosure is justified in the public interest. (*Initial Services Ltd.* v. *Putterill* [1968] 1 QB, 396   405)

In 1980 Lord Wilberforce held that the circumstances in which disclosure in the public interest might be justified: 'extends in fact beyond "iniquity" to misconduct generally'. (*British Steel Corporation* v. *Granada* [1980], 3 WLRD, 774, 821–2) The principle was endorsed by the Law Commission in its 1981 report which proposed giving the law of confidence a statutory basis. The Law Commission's draft 'Breach of Confidence Bill' incorporated a statutory public interest defence, defined as follows: 'A public interest may be involved in the disclosure or use of information notwithstanding that the information does not relate to any crime, fraud or other misconduct'. (*Breach of Confidence*, 1981, Cmnd 8388.)

This bill contained three simple propositions: a citizen should not be convicted and possibly imprisoned without independent review of a ministerial certificate that a serious injury to our national interest had taken place; secondly that the suppression of information indicating iniquity in government, that is crime, fraud or abuse of authority, is actually against the public interest; and thirdly that once official information, albeit in the protected categories, has escaped and become known, the British public has a right to be informed and in order to secure that right there would be a defence of prior publication.

In July 1988 the Government published its own White Paper on Reform of Section 2 of the Official Secrets Act, 1911 (cm 408). It addressed the first of our contentions by introducing absolute offences that do not require a ministerial certificate, and where the prosecution would have to meet a damage test lowering this test from 'serious injury' to in one instance a 'prejudice' test. The Government's White Paper dismisses both an iniquity defence and the defence of prior publication. It does not attempt to strike any balance between the proper requirements of national security and foreign relations, on the one hand, and of freedom of speech and of the press, on the other. It reflects the nostrums of Whitehall without weighing the experience of other democracies with similar institutions to our own such as Canada and Australia.

10 Local Government in the Firing Line

John Benington and Dr Gerry Stoker

Local government is currently the site of a fundamental battle of interests, ideas and values within British society. It is one of the present Government's main targets in their fight to displace the post-war consensus in support of a welfare state based on collective solutions to needs, and to substitute an alternative ideology based on the individual, the family and the private market. In seeking to do this the Government has resorted to an increasingly tight censorship of local authorities' role in the creation and dissemination of knowledge, ideas and values.

Central government has intervened against local government with increasing frequency and intensity throughout the 1980s. Since 1979 they have introduced over 46 separate Bills directed specifically against local authorities. However, commentators have perhaps not given sufficient attention to the underlying significance of this drive towards centralised control.

For the present Government's aim is not simply to curtail local authority expenditure, but to challenge and change the basis of local democracy itself. Their strategy is to restructure the conditions under which services are produced and distributed within society and to impose their own values. This kind of curb on local democracy amounts to a censorship over local authorities' freedom to act and even to express their views. It can also be seen in some cases as a censorship of the local electorate, riding roughshod over its democratically expressed wishes.

Whereas previous administrations aimed to control the overall size of local authority budgets, the present government has attempted to curtail specific aspects of local expenditure and to shift the balance of power over finance from local to central government – and wherever possible to pass financial control to the private sector.

Their initial argument for this unprecedented level of intervention was the need to restrain the growth in local authority expenditure. While it is true that local government expenditure had almost doubled as a share of GNP from 9.8 per cent in 1951 to 18.6 per cent in 1975, and governments of all political persuasions had tried to ·

impose restrictions, this Government has taken a much more fundamentalist line. On the one hand they have attacked the legitimacy of much local authority expenditure on the grounds that (like all public sector activity in their terms) it is parasitic on wealth which has to be created in the private sector. On the other hand they have attempted to redirect and redistribute local authority expenditure and activity into areas of activity which more closely match their interests and ideologies.

For nine years the Government has engaged in a long series of skirmishes to gain control over both the level and the direction of local government expenditures (for example, the introduction of grant-related expenditure assessments, targets, penalties, holdbacks, clawbacks, 'grant-related poundage schedule tapers' and of course ratecapping). The Government now appears to be retreating from its attempt to control spending, and is shifting its attention to controlling the income side of the local authority equation. Their new strategy focuses on controlling local government's two main sources of independent income: rate revenues and borrowing of capital.

The Local Government Finance Bill (its equivalent is already law in Scotland where its implementation is being fiercely opposed) plans to replace domestic rates with a community charge or poll tax levied on all adults, and to replace non-domestic rates with a centrally fixed and nationally uniform business rate. This will have the effect of reducing local authorities' independent locally raised income from the present level of over 50 per cent of total expenditure to no more than 20–25 per cent. Central government will thus have gained control over 75–80 per cent of local government revenue income.

On 7 July 1988 the Secretary of State for the Environment, Nicholas Ridley, announced new measures to control the amounts of capital which local councils can borrow. Previous measures have attempted to control how much capital local authorities can spend; but these have frequently been circumvented by various methods of 'creative accounting' which in effect increase the amount of capital which local authorities can spend, in the short term. The new moves are designed to prevent this by controlling how much capital local authorities can *borrow* let alone spend. This is in line with the government's monetarist theories.

The Poll Tax has been presented by the Tories as an opportunity for the local voter to gain more direct influence over expenditure by establishing a closer connection between the individual and the services paid for and received. This is largely illusory however because, as shown above, the proportion of local government income which will be raised locally will now be so much smaller; and because of the very decisive shift of control over local expenditure into the hands of central government.

In fact the centralisation of control goes even further in that the Local Government Finance Bill confers no less than 34 separate statutory powers on the Secretary of State himself. This, combined with the Government's tendency to introduce retrospective legislation, means that ministers can exercise very detailed control over specific areas of local authority expenditure and activity.

However, this Government's battle with local government is not only, nor even primarily, concerned with finance. Many of their own proposals are in fact quite costly. For example the extra costs of preparing to introduce the community charge are estimated by central government to total £110 million; and the additional costs of introducing compulsory competitive tendering or transferring responsibility for education from the ILEA to the London Boroughs are considerable.

The Government seek to gain control over and restructure local government services in line with their own interests and values. To do this they are willing to override local democracy wherever there is opposition. Their aim is to privatise as many services as possible; or to subject them to the commercial regulation of the private market; and to promote the concept of increased consumer choice and accountability through competition. This is a fundamental challenge to the welfare state principle that services are allocated on the basis of need rather than ability to pay, and that quality, choice and accountability are achieved by electing representatives rather than through the individual purchasing commodities within the market.

There are at least five major areas where the Government programme challenges the traditional roles and assumptions of elected local authorities:

1. Competitive Tendering
The 1980 Local Government, Planning and Land Act introduced competitive tendering for building works and maintenance. The 1988 Local Government Act goes further and compels councils to put a further seven services out to competitive tender: refuse collection, street cleaning, ground maintenance, cleaning of schools and other buildings, vehicle repair and maintenance, and catering (including school meals). The management of sports and leisure facilities has since been added to this list.

One of the disturbing features of this and other current government legislation is that the Act gives the Secretary of State the power at any time to add in this way to the list of defined activities which are subject to competitive tender. During the passage of the Act some MPs advocated another 32 areas of local government activity suitable for competitive tendering – including social services, burials and cremations! The most serious aspect, however, remains the shift of control over such fundamental decisions not only away from locally elected authorities, but also away from Parliament and into the hands of ministers. Competitive tendering could of course act as a salutary stimulus to local authorities to check that they are still providing services that meet community needs as efficiently and effectively as possible. However that does not appear to be the Government's goal.

It is hard to escape the impression that the real aim of the legislation is to open up potentially lucrative new markets for the private sector to explore and exploit. The expansion of local government activity since the war has created a relatively large sphere of collective consumption within the economy. As with the larger scale privatisation programme for the nationalised industries the Government's aim is to 'liberate' these public assets and social markets in order to create new business opportunities. Some local authority contracts are relatively risky (or at least unpredictable) for the private sector, but a cushion is provided for them by the fact that local authorities have been left with the statutory responsibility for ensuring that these services are provided at all, and for guaranteeing minimum standards. The private sector will thus be able to abandon markets and withdraw from contracts which do not prove profitable or viable. But local authorities will be left with a duty – they must ensure the continuation of the service.

The inequality between the public and private sectors in the Government's requirements for the tendering process is reinforced by the fact that local authorities are prevented from including any of their social responsibilities or commitments in their specification of the contracts. The legislation prevents local authorities from attaching any 'non-commercial' criteria (like terms and conditions of employment, training and promotion opportunities, use of sub-contracted or lump labour etc.). The only exception to this is that local authorities will have powers to withhold contracts from private firms as part of their duty to promote equality of opportunity between races.

2. Housing

One of the services which the present government is most keen to remove from local authority control is housing. Council tenants are to

be given the right to 'pick a landlord'. All council tenants will have a
chance to transfer the ownership of their home to another landlord –
a housing association, housing trust, co-operative or a private
landlord. In this situation the tenant is likely to face a higher rent
level. At the same time, however, council rents will be forced up by
government action.

All this is presented as an extension of choice for the tenant.
However it is hard not to see the measures as mainly designed to
make it more attractive for tenants to opt out of local authority
housing, and to undermine the role of local authorities in this field.
This is certainly evident in the proposals in the Housing Bill to allow
the Government to set up Housing Act Trusts (HATs) to take over
and sell off complete council estates. The prospect is that stripped of
overall housing control local authorities will once more be left with
the difficult and costly social responsibilities such as housing the
homeless, the disabled and poor.

3. Education

The Government's radical restructuring of the education service also
represents a fundamental challenge to the role of local authorities,
and to the basic principle of equality of educational opportunity on
which the service was founded. The proposal to allow schools to opt
out of local authority control and to take on, in effect, direct grant
status, together with the requirement that schools will not be allowed
to set any limit on admissions below their physical capacity, could
have a very divisive effect within the education system. It would
increase the disparity between popular and unpopular schools and
reinforce the inequality between privileged and underprivileged areas
and groups. Once again government reforms are presented in terms
of an increase in parental and user choice, but in practice are more
likely to result in a shift of control away from local authorities and
towards central government and the commercial sector. While school
governing bodies are to have increased responsibilities for budgets
and staffing delegated to them from local authorities, they will now
have to work within the framework of a national curriculum and
nationally determined tests. Although they will have greater representation from parents, both they and the local authorities will be
outnumbered by governors and co-optees from the business and
commercial world, though in Scotland there will be a majority of
parents on the school boards. Colleges of higher education will be
removed from local authority control altogether and run as independent corporations by academics and business representatives. The

Education Bill will also give central government power to make long term agreements with business sponsors for joint funding of city technology colleges which will concentrate on providing vocational and technical training.

What is at stake here is not simply who controls education – although that question has to be posed sharply when 350 new powers are to be vested directly in the Secretary of State for Education! The more fundamental issue is what values and ideas will inform education. Will a spirit of fearless critical enquiry undergird the education system at all levels, or will education be commercialised and 'privatised' in the sense that schools and colleges will be drawn primarily into matching the needs and value systems of the commercial and business world?

4. Economic Development

Another sphere of local government activity which has been in the firing line is economic development and urban regeneration. The Government's strategy is familiar – to impose a variety of legal and financial constraints on local authority involvement in these fields and to set up alternative machinery to bypass the elected authorities. The constraints in this case come via two White Papers from the Department of the Environment: 'Local Authorities' Interests in Companies (A Consultation Paper, June 1988)'; and 'The Conduct of Local Authority Business (the Government Response to the Report of the Widdicombe Committee of Enquiry, July 1988)'. The former limits the activities of companies under local authority control. The second restricts them to a new specific but 'circumscribed' power to engage in economic development. Between them they severely limit local authority power to initiate economic developments in the best interests of their area.

At the same time business and industrial interests have been given a greater influence over economic and urban development. But the removal of their investment decisions from the planning frameworks of an elected local authority is a further example of central government's attack on local democracy.

5. Library and Information Services

The Government has also published a Green Paper on 'The Financing of Public Library Services' (Cmnd 324 February 1988) which introduces draft proposals for the contracting out and competitive tendering of library and information services and the introduction of more charges for library and information services.

This has very far-reaching implications. The basis of democracy is an informed and thinking electorate, with the freedom to read what it wants, and to write and publish without restriction. The Green Paper emphasises that the Government is still committed to 'the free basic library service offered to individuals'. However it looks as if this basic service will be very basic indeed! Possible candidates for competitive tendering are listed as 'library services to local old people's homes, the provision of video tape lending services, and perhaps at a later stage the running of branch library services.' The danger is that, forced to operate within an increasingly commercial and competitive framework, the priorities of the library service will go to those aspects which generate most revenue, either because of their 'mass appeal' or because of their interest to commercial sponsors. The range of books and materials available to minority interests or to those who can't pay commercial fees would inevitably then diminish.

However, the Government is intent not just on bringing local authority library services within a more commercial and profit-conscious framework. They also want to influence the ideological content of the information disseminated more generally by local authorities. This is apparent both in Section 28 of the Local Government Act which prevents local authorities from 'intentionally promoting homosexuality', and in Section 27 which bans local authorities from publishing (or assisting others to publish) 'any material which, in whole or in part, appears to be designed to affect public support for a political party'. Several legal opinions have suggested that this clause does not widely extend the restrictions on councils' publicity powers, and will not make illegal anything that is not illegal under present law. However the definition of political is fairly broad. It includes material which 'promotes or opposes a point of view on a question of political controversy which is identifiable as the view of one political party and not of another'. This would appear to include any material promoting or opposing all the above legislation affecting local government. (Again, one thinks of the local authority opposition to the Poll Tax proposals in Scotland.) Indeed Section 27 is clearly designed primarily to suppress local opposition to the Government's programme. The Government has no intention of applying Section 27 to, for example, its own publicity campaigns for the Single European Market in 1992, for the restyled Department of Enterprise, or for the new programmes promoted by the Training Commission – although these are probably 'identifiable as the view of one political party and not of another'! The attempt to legislate against local authority publicity material on questions of political controversy is itself, of course, part of a wider battle of ideas in which this Government is an active protagonist.

The overall thrust of the new legislation, therefore, is to remove key areas of local government activity from local democratic control, and to expose an increasing range of services to privatisation or compulsory competitive tendering. The effect of this is to shift the balance of power in four main directions: from local to central government; from the political to the managerial arena by replacing elected representatives by non-elected bodies; from the public to the private sector; and replacing collective solutions to human needs by individualistic solutions via the market.

The strength of the Government's commitment to restructuring economic, social and class relations in Britain is paralleled by its determination to abolish centres of alternative ideas and values (for example, the GLC, the metropolitan counties and ILEA) and to depoliticise, bypass, or to render inoperable those aspects of local government which they oppose.

Several of the Government's initiatives are specifically aimed at repressing local authorities' freedom to promote and publicise certain kinds of ideas. The most obvious examples have already been mentioned – Sections 27 and 28 of the Local Government Act, 1988. There is however further legislation in the pipeline. It follows from the recommendations of the Widdicombe Committee, and the Government's response to it entitled 'The Conduct of Local Authority Business'. This will prevent senior council officials and other staff in sensitive positions from being councillors or engaging in public political activity; ban the appointment of party political advisers to a council's staff; and exclude councillors from involvement in the appointment of staff who are not within the proposed 'politically restricted' category.

The declared aim of these measures is to reassert the traditional distinction between policy-making and its implementation and to 'depoliticise' the process of management and administration within local government. The tone of the White Paper is fairly balanced and reasonable, and in several places less draconian than the Widdicombe Committee's own recommendations. However, it is not in the realm of the formal political structures and procedures that the really crucial battle of ideas and values is taking place. The Government's aim is not to remove politics in general from local government, but to repress the specific politics with which they disagree and to impose their own political and moral values. Their support for a national curriculum in schools; for the re-establishment of the Christian faith as the dominant form of religious education; for a particular approach to sex education and the role of the family in society: all embody particular political and moral value judgements. The aim is not therefore to depoliticise local government, but to 'repoliticise' it in accordance with their particular interests and ideologies.

This comes out clearly in their treatment of the question of co-options of non-elected people onto committees. In chapter 2 of their 'Response to Widdicombe' the Government agrees with the Committee that *'subject to particular exceptions*, non-elected persons should not be appointed by the council as voting members of decision-taking committees. This will make it clear to electors who is responsible for taking decisions on behalf of the council.'

The 'particular exceptions' the Government suggests are revealing! They include magistrates on police committees, and church representatives on education committees. In fact the paragraph (2,14a) which argues that teachers and other education professionals should *not* be co-opted onto education committees as voting members, announces that the Government proposes to *'require* councils to appoint representatives of those churches and any other organisations in the area who provide voluntary schools there as members of education committees with full voting rights.' We have already given similar examples earlier in this chapter of the Government's introduction of non-elected business and commercial interests into the governing bodies for schools, polytechnics and colleges of further education. All this is not only selective discrimination, but in the field of education, where ideas should be paramount, it adds up to a dangerous form of selective censorship.

The Government's attacks on local democracy are not merely designed to control expenditure, or to curtail activities of which they disapprove, or even simply to abolish or demolish centres of political opposition or autonomy. All these are part of the Government's declared aims. However there is a more fundamental reason why local government is at the very centre of the target for the whole 'New Right' project in the 1980s. Local government has been at the heart of the post-war welfare state. It has been one of the main mechanisms for redistribution of resources and opportunities within British society: one of the central channels for the development and delivery of services to match communal needs; and therefore in many ways the custodian of the political ideas and values that lie behind the whole notion of a 'welfare state'. Its direct involvement in the development of key services like education, housing, social services, public health, planning, leisure and recreation has meant it has become almost the embodiment of the values and vision of the welfare state. To be sure, these values have frequently become obscured and the vision distorted. Nevertheless local government has been one of the main repositories of Beveridge's basic principles of universal services, provided as of right, through a democratic state financed communally through taxation.

The New Right are promoting a radical alternative vision: one in which needs are to be met primarily through the private market. In order to do this they have to displace the welfare state (and therefore local government) from its central position within the expenditure, activity and ideology of British society, and replace it with a fundamentally different concept of what might be called the enterprise state.

The fundamental battle of ideas around these alternative concepts of the role of the state goes a long way to explaining why local government is in the front line of the Government's radical programme for restructuring British society. However, the battle is not just at the level of popular consciousness, that is, a battle to win the hearts and minds of the electorate. It is also a very concrete battle to determine what interests shape the future direction of British society as we confront profound structural changes and choices.

We are witnessing the beginning of a third industrial revolution based on computer aided design and manufacture and robotised manufacturing systems (for example, for small-batch production and customised products for specialised markets). Major technological and industrial changes of this kind often have major implications not just for employment but also for patterns of communication and social interaction. The new generation of information systems, based upon the linking of computing and telecommunications, open up the possibility of widespread interactive communication networks. This could amount to a revolution as profound as that brought about by steelbased technologies in the past. This poses profound choices about the uses to which the new information and communication systems are to be put, about the interests they are to serve, and the kind of society they are to foster. Democracy depends on the freedom to think and to communicate ideas. Access to information therefore gives access to power. The new communication systems can either be used to extend democratic access to information through open networks, or they can be used to concentrate control over information even more centrally, among the power elites.

At the same time demographic changes like the ageing of the

population, and cultural changes like the growth of the women's movement and the various ethnic minorities also pose profound questions about values, and choices about priorities for resource allocation.

It is not surprising, therefore, that many of these issues have found their way onto the agenda of local authority debate and action. But they cannot be tackled simply through the delivery of existing services: local authorities have therefore been forced to go beyond their limited service-delivery role, and to explore new forms of investigation, innovation and intervention. In doing so, many local authorities have discovered that they have two additional sources of power in addition to their traditional social role as distributors of services. They have a potentially important economic role arising from their importance locally as major employers, investors, purchasers and business operators. They also have a very significant ideological role arising from the fact that the local council is elected democratically to represent the needs and interests of the whole local community. Councils which recognise their potential in this role have found that they can play a major part in influencing the thinking and action of other local organisations and their electorate at large.

In conclusion, therefore, we see that the New Right's attack on local government is part of a very fundamental battle of interests and ideas about what kind of society we are going to build, as we move through a period of profound economic, technological, demographic and social change. Local government in many ways embodies the values and the vision of the welfare state, a model of society as a community of citizens making provision for their needs through authorities and agencies accountable to them collectively through their elected representatives. The New Right however aims radically to restructure British society on a very different model: as a market of consumers purchasing individual services and insurances to meet their own needs as far as possible through private competitive agencies, accountable to them individually in their role as consumer, or through self-help and the nuclear family. It is not surprising therefore that local government is in the centre of the firing line, and that the Government is so determined to control and redirect local authority finance and services. It is because of this that it seeks also censor the role of local democracy as a creator and distributor of knowledge, ideas and values.

11 *Spycatcher*: My Country Wright or Armstrong?

Heather Rogers

Freedom of speech is always the first casualty under a totalitarian regime. Such a regime cannot afford to allow the free circulation of information and ideas among its citizens. Censorship is the indispensable tool to regulate what the public may and what they may not know. The present attempt to insulate the public in this country from information which is freely available elsewhere is a significant step down that very dangerous road.

This was a contemporary description of the Government's attempts to suppress newspaper reports of Peter Wright's book *Spycatcher*. They are not the words of a newspaper editor, or of a political polemicist. They are taken from the dissenting speech of Lord Bridge in the House of Lords judgment in August 1987.

These extraordinary words were used because of the Government's relentless pursuit of a ban on publication of the Wright book. No matter that Wright made serious allegations about the conduct of the security service. No matter that one million copies of his book were sold worldwide. The British public had no right to know what he said.

The state of the law in Britain today favours the suppression of information. Although the Government no longer uses the criminal law to punish the disclosure of official information, the civil law offers ample remedies. Recent developments have left the press and the public in a lamentable position.

The existence of a wide-ranging law which can be used at the whim of the executive creates an atmosphere of repression. Where anyone can be prosecuted or faced with an injunction, everyone is at risk. Harassment of the media becomes commonplace. Sackfuls of threatening letters are sent by the Treasury Solicitor. Craven apologists for the government are fed information which they can safely publish. Critics seeking to publish the same information face legal action. Stories are not written because the legal risks are not worth running.

The present state of the law does not protect the legitimate function of a free press in a democracy – to be the eyes and ears of the public.

THE CRIMINAL LAW

The Official Secrets Act 1911 rushed through all its Parliamentary stages in one day during a rash of spy fever. Section 1 was intended to deal with traitors and spies, carrying out activities 'prejudicial to the interests of the state'. The 'catch-all' Section 2, not debated at all, was meant to keep information secret. It is very broad in scope and creates a large number of criminal offences concerned with the communication, use or receipt of official information.

Section 2 was described as 'a mess' by the Franks Committee in 1972 and has been criticised by all the major political parties. Although its use was discredited, prosecutions continued. As Attorney General between 1979 and 1987 Michael Havers used it more frequently than his predecessors. But his targets were not journalists, who might fight cases on an issue of principle. By prosecuting the source instead, it was hoped that the guilty party would go quietly. In 1984 Sarah Tisdall, a lowly Ministry of Defence clerk who had leaked documents to the *Guardian*, did just that. Tisdall pleaded guilty and was given the clearly deterrent sentence of six months' imprisonment.

The trial in 1985 of Clive Ponting, the Ministry of Defence civil servant who admitted passing material on the sinking of the *Belgrano* to MP Tam Dalyell, was strongly contested. Ponting's only defence was that his action was 'in the interests of the state'. The judge, Mr Justice McCowan, decided that, by legal definition, the 'interests of the state' meant the interests of the government of the day. Whatever the government's policy was at any time *was* the interests of the state. For a moment Ponting's prospects looked bleak. But the judge could not direct the jury to convict and the jury took just two hours to acquit.

The Ponting acquittal in February 1985 was described by many who had not heard the evidence as a 'perverse' jury verdict. But the case showed the fundamental problem faced by a government using the criminal law to protect its information – a jury decides where the public interest lies. No matter what the prosecution may say, or how the judge might define the law, it is the jury who will decide on the relative importance of protecting information and of disclosure.

After the Ponting verdict, it was plain that the Government could not trust a jury to convict just because a civil servant had disclosed official information to an unauthorised person. But the jury, the vital safeguard of democracy, has no place in the civil law and it was to the civil law that the government would go to establish and enforce a broad principle of secrecy. It would invoke the law of breach of confidence to muzzle the media.

SPYCATCHER AND THE LAW OF CONFIDENCE

Peter Wright was employed as an officer in the British security service, MI5, from 1955 to 1976. At the time he left he was on the personal staff of the Director General of the service. He was convinced that the former Director General, Sir Roger Hollis, had been a Soviet agent. After he retired to Tasmania Wright gave information to the writer, Chapman Pincher. Pincher's book *Their Trade is Treachery* was published in 1981. The Government took no action to ban it.

Wright was dissatisfied with the book's conclusion that all was right with the intelligence world. He prepared and sent a dossier to Anthony Kershaw, Chairman of the Foreign Affairs Select Committee, who passed it to the Cabinet Secretary, Sir Robert Armstrong. Again nothing happened. In 1984 Wright appeared on the Granada television programme *The Spy Who Never Was*. The Government made no attempt to stop him or the broadcast. Wright then decided to write a book. It was this book that led to court actions around the world – with the British taxpayer footing the bill.

The first proceedings began in Australia in September 1985. Peter Wright and his publishers agreed not to publish the book until after the end of the trial. A long series of pre-trial applications and manoeuvres began.

In June 1986 in Britain, two newspapers, the *Guardian* and the *Observer*, published short reports about the Australian proceedings. Each set out some of the allegations made in the Wright book. These included bugging of embassies contrary to international conventions, an MI6 plot to assassinate President Nasser, and an MI5 plot to destabilise the Labour Government of Harold Wilson. The response of the Attorney General was swift. He obtained injunctions preventing the newspapers from publishing any information derived from Peter Wright, or attributing any information to him.

The basis of the action in Australia and of the injunctions in Britain was the law of confidence. Its origins were far removed from the world of spies and government. It all began with Prince Albert's etchings. When Queen Victoria's consort took his etchings to an engraver to be reproduced, the unscrupulous man attempted to produce and sell more copies. The court prevented this. The etchings had been handed over in confidence and the engraver had no right to use them for his own purposes.

This principle was developed by the courts mainly through commercial cases, to protect trade secrets or scientific developments. No employer would invest in research and development if ex-employees could set up in competition, making use of secret business methods or confidential lists of customers. In such cases the court weighs the public interest in the preservation of confidence against the public interest in people being free to practice their trade. Only 'reasonable' restraints are enforced.

There are two essential elements in an action for breach of confidence: confidential information and a duty of confidence. Where confidential information is communicated in circumstances importing an obligation of confidence, the court will restrain the 'confidee' from using the 'confider's' information. The information is treated as the private property of the confider, who can control its use. If the confidee passes the information to third parties, the confider can restrain them too. Anyone who obtains confidential information knowing that there has been a breach of confidence is liable.

Some types of information and some types of relationship are always treated as confidential. For example, a doctor may not reveal what he knows about a patient's medical history. The law also gives a special recognition to the relationship of marriage. Although the regular revelations in the tabloid press would suggest otherwise, the law in principle requires that private communications passing between husband and wife remain secret. Even if the marriage breaks down in acrimonious circumstances, one spouse cannot get revenge on the other by telling all to the press.

INJUNCTIONS AND GOVERNMENT INFORMATION

The general principles of the law of breach of confidence apply also to civil servants. Like all other employees, civil servants owe a duty of good faith to their employer. This prevents them from leaking information to the press, or from publishing it themselves. It is not affected by the routine practice which requires all government employees to sign an Official Secrets Act declaration. This merely emphasises the cult of secrecy that exists in the government service.

There were until recently very few examples of the Government using the law of confidence, but now, worryingly, the number of actions is increasing. The first reported case concerned the Attorney General's attempt in 1974 to prevent publication of Richard Crossman's Cabinet Diaries. He argued that all cabinet discussions were confidential and publication would destroy the mutual trust required for the efficient working of cabinet. Lord Chief Justice Widgery decided that an injunction could be granted to prevent the publication of such confidential information, but only if it were strictly necessary in the public interest and if there were no countervailing interests in favour of publication. Only such restraint as was strictly necessary would be imposed. No injunction was necessary in this case.

The Crossman Diaries were published. Since then many diaries and books by other cabinet ministers and senior officials have been published. The Attorney General's fears were unfounded. Cabinet government has survived!

The principle laid down by Lord Chief Justice Widgery in the Crossman Diaries case has been accepted in the Australian courts. They say governments are not in the same position as individuals and the court should look at a government application for an injunction 'through different spectacles'. The fact that publicity would open government activity to public discussion or cause embarrassment was not sufficient reason upon which to found an injunction. There would be no injunction unless the public interest required it.

When a breach of confidence claim is made, almost all plaintiffs ask for an immediate injunction to prevent any publication until the case can be tried. This 'interlocutory injunction' is meant to be a temporary measure, to preserve the rights of the parties pending trial. At this early stage the balance is heavily in favour of granting an injunction. If an order is made wrongly (because the right to publish is established at trial), all that is lost is some delay in publication. But if the court wrongly allows publication, the confidence is lost forever. Nothing can be done to restore it. Weighed against such potential hardship to the confider, courts treat the delay to the publisher as trivial. But this approach ignores the reality of the situation.

In most breach of confidence actions there is no trial. The grant or refusal of an interlocutory injunction decides the case. If no injunction is granted, it is not worthwhile for the confider to go on with the case. If an injunction is granted, the publisher faces a long and expensive legal action to have it removed. Very few stories are worth the expense and delay of the legal process. The *Spycatcher* injunctions have prevented publication for more than two years and have cost the newspapers hundreds of thousands of pounds. It is small wonder that, in practice, most interlocutory injunctions continue forever.

It is much easier to obtain an injunction against the media in confidence than in libel. There is a long-standing rule in libel cases that the courts will not grant an injunction to prevent the publication of information which the publisher claims is true. The law recognises that the individual's right to reputation competes with the public interest in freedom of speech. Where truth is alleged the interest in free speech prevails and there can be no restraint. But there is no such rule in cases of breach of confidence. Truth is irrelevant.

It is not surprising, therefore, that the Government has found interlocutory injunctions to be a useful and effective ban on publication. Jock Kane, an employee of Government Communications Headquarters, GCHQ, in Hong Kong, wrote a book about its waste and inefficiency. He had complained to his superiors and to those who nominally exercised political control but nothing was done. In March 1984 the Attorney General obtained an injunction to stop publication of his book *GCHQ: The Negative Asset*. The publishers either could not afford to, or did not, take the matter to trial. That injunction still prevents the British public from hearing about Mr Kane's concerns today. (However, the Government itself had to allow publication of material about CGHQ in the report of the Security Commission after the conviction for spying of employee, Geoffrey Prime.)

An interlocutory injunction also prevents publication of Joan Miller's book *One Girl's War* which detailed her wartime experiences in MI5. But anyone can obtain a copy of the book by going to Dublin where government action failed because of the constitutional guarantee of free speech. However, even this anomaly pales into insignificance beside the absurd and extraordinary consequences of the Peter Wright injunctions.

Of course, the law has always recognised some competing interest in confidence cases. There is no confidence in 'iniquity', say the courts. No one can restrain the publication of information which discloses crimes, corruption or wrongdoing. The courts also accept that there are some matters which the public has a legitimate right to know. In such cases, the right of confidence will be outweighed and publication allowed. But in only one case has this principle been applied to refuse an interlocutory injunction. In most cases, the public interest in favour of publication will be considered only at the trial, when all the evidence is available.

In any event, the iniquity defence is not an unlimited guarantee of freedom of speech. Where there is information which suggests wrongdoing, the courts say that only the 'proper authorities' should be notified; the information should be given just to the police or other responsible body to investigate, not to the media or to the public; the media have no right to expose the allegations; the public should not be told. This is a severe limitation on freedom of speech where official information is concerned.

SECRECY AND THE SECURITY SERVICE

In the *Spycatcher* case, the Government argued that total secrecy is necessary for the efficient functioning of the security service, MI5. The only official definition of the role of MI5 is given by the Maxwell Fyfe Directive, a short, six-paragraph document issued by the Home Secretary in 1952. The Directive was prompted by an internal Whitehall dispute about MI5's place in the administrative hierarchy and it gives guidance about MI5's role only incidentally. MI5's task is said to be the defence of the realm as a whole from espionage, sabotage, and subversion; it is required to be free of political bias; its work is to be strictly limited to its task. But the law gives no special powers to MI5 employees and indeed Lord Denning in his report on the Profumo affair stressed that they are 'ordinary citizens'.

MI5 and the other 'secret departments', MI6 (the special intelligence service) and GCHQ, have an anomalous status. They are not accountable to Parliament and are left largely to run themselves. There is no good justification for this unique special status and lack of accountability. Every other Western democracy has taken steps to establish some kind of non-executive control. In Britain, the only steps are towards suppression of all information about their operations.

The injunctions obtained in England against the *Guardian* and *Observer* in June 1986 prevented them from publishing any information derived from Peter Wright, or attributing any information to him. This was a novel extension to the law of confidence. The injunction went beyond the protection of information which belonged to the 'confiding' Government. It prevented the attribution to Peter Wright of *any* information, true or false, whether belonging to the Government or not. The Government's approach is that to report anything as having been said by a serving or former member of the security service is damaging to the public interest.

The injunction allowed the newspapers to repeat information which had already been published by Wright on television or in Pincher's books or which was revealed in open court in Australia. When the injunctions were taken to the Court of Appeal in July 1986, the court added further exemptions, necessary to ensure that proceedings in Parliament and in United Kingdom courts could be reported freely. At least this small recognition was given to the role of the press.

THE AUSTRALIAN PROCEEDINGS

In Australia the trial at last began on 17 November 1986. Sir Robert Armstrong, Secretary to the Cabinet, had sworn four affidavits in support of the Government's case. The central argument was that Britain would be damaged in the eyes of her allies in the international intelligence world if Wright's book were published. Books by 'insiders' (members of the security service) simply could not be allowed; *any* information they published was damaging. That was why the government refused to 'blue pencil' the book. It was impossible to identify specific information that caused damage. Sir Robert stated that it was the government's 'consistent practice and policy' that no information relating to the security and intelligence services should ever be published, except with the authorisation of the Government.

It was clear from the start that Sir Robert was in for a rough ride from defence solicitor Malcolm Turnbull. Turnbull produced a large number of books already published about the security service, based on 'inside' information. All contained names of officers and descriptions of operations. Some even contained direct quotations attributed to security service members. Sir Robert could not explain why no action had been taken to prevent publication of these books. Nor could he explain why no action had been taken when former MI5 officers had appeared on television programmes. Sir Robert claimed that the *policy* of the Government was consistent, but admitted that its *practice* was not the same in every case.

Sir Robert maintained that nothing should be published, despite the fact that Australia, America and Canada all impose democratic accountability on their security services and have a practice of allowing publication of memoirs by former officers after clearance. The absurd insistence on absolute secrecy by the British establishment was shown when Sir Robert even refused to accept that MI6 existed. This devasting exposure of Britain's obsession with secrecy in a foreign court caused great amusement to the world's media.

Mr Justice Powell, the New South Wales Supreme Court judge, was known to be a conservative. He criticised the Government's 'serpentine weavings' and 'mumbo jumbo' in the running of the case. Sir Robert, he said, was only an official relying on what he was told. He could not give 'hard, detailed, compelling evidence'. Sir Robert's briefing had not been a full one. On a crucial matter of fact he had to retract evidence that had been incorrect; he apologised if he had, unwittingly, misled the court. On another occasion, caught off-guard in cross-examination, Sir Robert joked – with a now famous reply that he had been 'economical with the truth'.

The trial was finished in time for Christmas 1986. Meanwhile in the UK, journalist Duncan Campbell had been preparing a series of six programmes for the BBC entitled *Secret Society*. In January 1987 the BBC banned the broadcast of one of these programmes, concerned with the £500m Zircon satellite project which had not, contrary to a Ministry of Defence undertaking, been disclosed to the Public Accounts Committee. The Government obtained an injunction on the basis of the evidence of the Director of GCHQ, Peter Marychurch. As in *Spycatcher*, it was said that disclosure of any information would damage relations with the USA. The injunction was served on Duncan Campbell, but too late to prevent publication of the details of the programme in *New Statesman*. That edition sold out. The incompetence of the Government in failing to prevent publication was criticised heavily.

There was nothing unusual about the application for and grant of the injunction. What was surprising was the Government's next step. The Treasury Solicitor, head of the Government's legal service, wrote to editors of national newspapers seeking assurances that they would not publish anything covered by the injunction against Campbell. The newspapers refused. That injunction did not legally bind them. But Mrs Thatcher voiced the Government's concern that it was not possible to obtain a blanket injunction to stop all publication by the whole media. This was a problem to which the Government would return.

The Government's attempt to preserve the absolute secrecy of the secret departments continued into 1987. In March for example, the Government obtained an injunction preventing former GCHQ officer Dennis Mitchell from publishing anything he had learned during his 32 years at GCHQ. And meanwhile in Sydney, following Mr Justice Powell's decision to allow publication of *Spycatcher*, the Government immediately announced its intention to appeal and the injunctions were continued. The contents of Wright's manuscript of *Spycatcher* were still secret.

But in April 1987 the *Independent* newspaper obtained a copy of the manuscript. It published Wright's main allegations on the front page. The story was followed up by other newspapers and television companies in the UK and around the world. The Government was again swift to act. But this time the Attorney General did not use the law of confidence. He now began proceedings for contempt of court.

The law of contempt is a broadly based principle governing any conduct which interferes with the due administration of justice. Though it can take, and has taken, many different forms, this new application was totally unprecedented. It was based on the continuing existence of the 1986 interlocutory injunctions against the *Guardian* and *Observer*. The court had decided to 'hold the ring' in that case until trial. The Attorney General argued that by publishing Wright's allegations, the *Independent* had destroyed the confidentiality of the information and 'thwarted' the court's order. The function of the court, to decide whether or not the information should be published, was thereby usurped.

This application exposes to criticism the role of the Attorney General. In deciding whether or not to use the law of confidence to prevent publication of a book, the Attorney General is enforcing a private right held by the Crown. He is a member of government and acts on its behalf. He is entitled to take into account the views of other government ministers. However, the Attorney General also has another hat, which, in theory, is non-political. He has a duty to enforce the law. Wearing that hat he decides whether or not to prosecute under the Official Secrets Act. The decision to take action for contempt of court is, in theory, an exercise of this independent law-enforcing function. By an accident of the constitution the

Attorney General can use his second 'independent' role to support government action.

The Vice-Chancellor, Sir Nicolas Browne-Wilkinson, senior judge of the Chancery Division of the High Court, decided that publication in these circumstances could never amount to contempt of court. He said that the Attorney General's attempt to extend the law of criminal contempt would 'subvert the basic principles' of the civil law and introduce 'uncertainty and unfairness'. The Official Secrets Act provided criminal sanctions. Private rights should not be bolstered by contempt in an attempt to create a 'judge-made public law protecting official secrets'.

The Government appealed to the Court of Appeal. The court compared confidential information to an ice cube, which could easily melt and be destroyed. The court's function in confidence cases was to preserve the ice cube pending trial. Master of the Rolls, Sir John Donaldson said that it 'stuck in his gullet' that newspapers could go around interfering with the course of justice. The court's decision to protect confidential information could be effective only if an injunction bound everyone.

In giving judgment, Sir John gave a clear warning to all newspapers: *any* publication of information derived from or attributed to Peter Wright *could* be a contempt of court.

The implications of this judgment are the most damaging result (so far) of the *Spycatcher* legal saga. Before this case, injunctions bound only the parties directly involved in an action. Now, injunctions have a general effect. Anyone who knows of an injunction *may* be liable if they publish confidential information covered by the order. The penalties are, as in criminal cases, a fine or imprisonment yet there are none of the safeguards of a criminal trial and, most importantly, no jury. The judges alone decide where the public interest lies.

This is a very significant and highly dangerous fetter on free speech in cases involving government information. When an injunction is in force, the Attorney General has complete discretion about when and against whom to take action for this kind of contempt. The Attorney General has been criticised for using his power to prosecute under the Official Secrets Act for political ends. The contempt power is open to similar abuse. Friends of government may be left to publish safely, while critics are prosecuted. To avoid abuse, the 'political' and 'legal' functions of the Attorney General must be separated.

In the middle of all this, on 14 July 1987 Viking Penguin, an American subsidiary of the UK Pearson publishing group, released

Spycatcher in the USA. The Government had been advised that there was no possibility of a court ban in the USA because of the constitutional guarantee of free speech. The Treasury Solicitor had written letters, unsuccessfully, to pressurise Pearson into stopping publication. *Spycatcher* went on sale throughout the USA and hundreds of thousands of copies were sold. Copies soon began to arrive in the UK. Mrs Thatcher announced that no import ban was to be imposed on the book because it was unlikely to be effective. But this acceptance of the reality of the situation did not extend to the Government's attitude to the injunctions.

In July 1987 the Vice-Chancellor discharged the year-old injunctions after an application by the newspapers. 'In the contemporary world of electronics and jumbo jets, news anywhere is news everywhere', he said. In all the circumstances, the Spycatching cat was definitely out of the bag. The Government disagreed with his conclusion that the injunctions served no useful purpose any more and appealed. The Court of Appeal, led again by Sir John Donaldson, decided on a middle course and imposed a new injunction preventing anything other than a 'summary of the allegations in very general terms'. This compromise pleased no one and the case went to the House of Lords.

At the same time as the sitting of the House of Lords, the New South Wales Court of Appeal was hearing the Government's Australian appeal. As background to the hearings, extracts from *Spycatcher* had been published in the *Independent*, in the *Sunday Times*, and in newspapers throughout the world. The book itself was on sale in America and copies were flooding into Britain.

During the English hearing Lord Brandon said that the Government's intention was to impose the same kind of censorship as the Soviet Government, with banned books smuggled into the country. Yet he joined with the majority (with Lords Templeman and Ackner) in re-imposing the injunctions on 31 July 1987. Lords Bridge and Oliver, the minority, were in favour of lifting the injunction.

Indeed, their Lordships added a new restriction to the injunction. The newspapers were no longer to be free to report events in open court in Australia, but only the judgments. Incredibly, it was even suggested there should be no exemption to allow publication of reports of discussions in Parliament. This proposal, fortunately, was rejected.

So, the interlocutory injunctions were to continue despite the widespread publication of the book. The British public could not be allowed to read information about the British security service which had already been published all over the world. Any law which showed such scant regard for free speech, and gave rise to the ludicrous spectacle of attempting to prevent the reading of a book which was being widely read, was plainly an ass.

The Law Lords gave reasons for the decision in August 1987. Lord Bridge, former head of the Security Commission, said that it was 'manifestly too late' for the injunctions to protect national security. Anyone could buy the book in America and bring it home. Using the words set out at the beginning of this essay, Lord Bridge said that his confidence in the capacity of the common law (judge-made law) to safeguard the fundamental freedoms essential to a free society had been 'seriously undermined' by this case.

Although there is no constitutional guarantee of free speech in this country, unlike the USA or Ireland, the UK is party to the European Convention on Human Rights. Article 10 of the Convention, which guarantees free speech, states that the exercise of freedom of expression:

> may be subject to such ... restrictions ... as are prescribed by law and are necessary in a democratic society, in the interests of national security ... for the protection of the reputation or rights of others, for preventing the disclosure of information received in confidence or for maintaining the authority and impartiality of the judiciary.

It is doubtful whether a formal guarantee of free speech in these terms, with exemptions which are open to a broad interpretation, would have made any difference. Indeed, Lord Templeman found that the continuation of the injunctions was necessary in a democratic society for all the purposes listed above as exceptions to article 10. His attitude is in marked contrast to that of Coke, Blackstone and those judges in the past who jealously guarded rights of freedom of speech and preserved the liberties of the citizen against the excesses of the government.

Following the American publication of *Spycatcher* the world's press had taken up the story. The Government promptly obtained injunctions preventing press publication in Hong Kong and New Zealand. It was powerless in Canada, where the book went on sale. In September, the New South Wales Court of Appeal delivered judgment, allowing publication of the book. The Government made its final appeal to the High Court of Australia. On 29 September 1987 that court lifted the injunction restraining publication of *Spycatcher*. *Spycatcher*, which had been at the top of the American best seller lists for some weeks, could at last be published in Australia.

The case had taken two years.

Back home in England, the case against the *Guardian*, *Observer*, and, now, the *Sunday Times* came to trial in November 1987. The Government argued for an absolute duty of secrecy to be imposed on all members of the security and intelligence services; the disclosure of any information by such people was inevitably damaging – no matter how old the information or how trivial. The Government said it would be unlikely to act if someone revealed the menu of the MI5 canteen – but that would nevertheless be a breach of confidence. The duty of secrecy should continue even after information was made public.

The Government's argument was that newspapers had no role to play in the field of the security service. It maintained a number of rigid propositions: informed public debate was impossible. The press should not build up public pressure. The press should always go to the authorities and wait for their investigations. The Government explicitly stated that there was no room for arguments about press freedom in this field. There should be a system of prior restraint. Anyone wishing to publish should ask for permission from the Treasury Solicitor or the courts.

Sir Robert Armstrong, a shadow of the man who gave evidence in Australia, gave evidence again for the Government. He had spent the previous week giving similar evidence in the New Zealand trial. Although he conceded that *Spycatcher* was no longer secret after a million copies had been sold, he contended that further publication was still damaging.

Mr Justice Scott dismissed the Government's argument for an absolute ban on publication of information. This could not be achieved 'this side of the Iron Curtain'. Some of Wright's allegations were plainly iniquitous, and whether they were true or false, the public had a right to know about them. The court had to conduct a balance to decide whether the interest of free speech or the preservation of confidence should prevail.

The Government appealed. Unusually, a date for the appeal had been set before Mr Justice Scott gave judgment.

MORE INJUNCTIONS

Over the New Year period government lawyers, ever sleepless in their vigilance, obtained new injunctions to prevent newspapers from publishing *Inside Intelligence*, the memoirs of former MI6 officer, Anthony Cavendish. However, it was possible to 'blue pencil' that text to allow publication of part of the book. The Scottish courts later refused to grant injunctions, so that Scots newspapers were free to publish the book. (See chapter 12.)

Then the Government struck again. This time the Attorney General obtained an extremely wide ranging injunction preventing the BBC from publishing *any* information obtained from *any* security or intelligence service officers. BBC Radio Four had produced a series called *My Country, Right or Wrong* in which several former members of MI5, MI6 and GCHQ were interviewed. An injunction was granted although the programmes had already been cleared in principle by the Secretary to the D-Notice Committee (a body which represents both media and government interests and advises what information in the defence and security fields can be published safely). The ban covered all of the BBC's programmes. Strictly, they could not even refer to Peter Wright or his allegations which had been revealed in open court. Because of the contempt ruling, everyone else was bound too. In classic doublethink, Attorney General Patrick Mayhew announced in Parliament that this was 'not a question of censorship'.

At about the same time, in December 1987, a sweeping injunction had been ordered against Duncan Campbell. He was ordered to hand over all documents he had obtained from GCHQ employees. He was not to publish any information about GCHQ and was to hand over to the Government a list of all those persons to whom he had passed the information. Unsurprisingly, the Attorney General announced that there would be no Official Secrets Act prosecution. The fear of British juries still prevailed.

Back with *Spycatcher*, on the last day of the Court of Appeal hearing in January 1988, the Attorney General asked the court for an order which would ban the publication of:

> any material obtained by any member or former member of the British Security and Intelligence Services in his capacity as a member thereof and which they know, or have reasonable ground to believe, to have come or been obtained whether directly or indirectly, from such other member or former member of the said services.

This injunction bore no relation to Wright's disclosures. It would simply and absolutely prohibit the publication of any intelligence information. The Government argued strongly that it should not be required to show in each case why it was important to protect particular information. Preservation of the principle of confidentiality was enough.

During the hearing, Master of the Rolls, Sir John Donaldson, expressed extraordinary views about the powers of the security service. He said that it was 'silly to sit here and say that the security service must follow the letter of the law: it isn't real'. He added that the security service could not get by without bugging and burgling; it was proper that they should not be prosecuted for any offences except, perhaps, for murder. (In his judgment, after discussing the case with Lords Justice Bingham and Dillon, Sir John accepted that physical violence would not be an 'excusable' breach of the law.) There is, of course, no legal basis for giving MI5 officers such a privileged position. Sir John also made it plain that he thought no information about the security service should be published. There was the plainest public interest, he said, that the public should not know of an allegation, even if true, that MI5 planned to assassinate a foreign head of state. This suggests that the courts should strive to maintain public confidence in the security service even if there are no grounds for such confidence.

The Court of Appeal decision was given in February 1988. The court agreed that there was no legal basis on which it could grant the general injunction sought by the government. Because of the widespread publication of *Spycatcher*, any injunction would be 'futile'. The book could be published. However, the temporary injunctions would continue until an appeal to the House of Lords.

The Court of Appeal stated the important conclusion that the duty of confidence owed by members of the security service was *not* absolute. Like everyone else, they could disclose wrongdoing or iniquity. Newspapers could publish such information if they had a credible source and carried out all possible independent checks. They should take into account any possible harm that might be caused, and consider any investigations which have been carried out. But they need not be able to prove that the allegations were true.

It is an important safeguard for the press that newspapers are not required to prove that actual wrongdoing took place. In this field they simply could not obtain the information. Normally in breach of confidence actions the parties exchange all relevant documents on 'discovery'. The government in this case would refuse to do so on the grounds of 'public interest immunity'. Such a claim would be raised by the Attorney General wearing his 'guardian of the public interest' hat, *not* as plaintiff in the action. The government would also try to prevent the media from calling any witnesses from MI5. In the *Spycatcher* trial in November 1987, the Government had filed a certificate from Home Secretary Douglas Hurd stating that it would be contrary to the public interest for anyone to give evidence about their work in the security service, or even to be identified as members of the security service. The government will try at any cost to prevent such evidence from being given in court, even behind closed doors. Arguments about public interest immunity have the other advantage for the government of being costly. They would delay any trial.

FINAL APPEAL

In June 1988 five more Law Lords heard the *Spycatcher* case (Lords Keith, Griffith, Goff, Brightman and Jauncey). By that time, more than a million copies of *Spycatcher* had been sold. It was available in Ireland and in Europe, as well as America, Canada, Australia and New Zealand. Yet the government still asked that the British press be restrained from publishing any information from *Spycatcher*. The Attorney General produced another new formula for a general injunction in a last attempt to achieve a judicial blanket ban.

The court appeared sympathetic to the idea of creating a machinery for vetting proposed publications of information about the security service. There was a clear reluctance to trust the press. Lord Griffith stressed the desirability of 'bright lines' to guide the press. The hearing finished in June 1988, but after the overwhelming criticism of the hasty 3:2 decision in July 1987, their Lordships took time for lengthy deliberations. The decision was not expected until October 1988. It will reveal how their Lordships manage to reconcile the desire to control the press with the fact that the introduction by the judiciary of a system of prior restraint runs counter to all established legal principle.

Meanwhile, by July 1988, the BBC had been allowed to broadcast *My Country, Right or Wrong*. The Treasury Solicitor had withdrawn his objections to the programmes, but only after transcripts had been given to him. The BBC had also announced that it would broadcast the *Zircon* programme. Although this had led to wide injunctions and to several extensive searches by Special Branch under Official Secrets Act warrants, the Treasury Solicitor assured the BBC that there was no damage to national security. The BBC's ability to broadcast the programme will not, apparently, be a contempt of court, despite the existence of the injunction against Duncan Campbell. The Attorney General's actions for contempt of court against the *Independent* and six other selected newspapers were still going through preliminary hearings at the time of going to press.

The whole dreadful *Spycatcher* saga illustrates the bizarre lengths to which the Government will go to keep from the British public information freely available in the rest of the world. In a world of international satellite communications it is both futile and absurd to try to insulate Britain in this way. The law of confidence ought to recognise that once information is published anywhere, it ceases to be confidential everywhere.

So far, the courts have refused to accept the Government's argument that a duty of confidence can impose absolute secrecy. Information which reveals serious wrongdoing *may* be published. The public can be told and the government cannot restrain publication. The judges have recognised that the media have a role to play. As Lord Justice Bingham put it, in the Court of Appeal in February 1988, 'freedom of the press is not an optional extra'.

But other important constitutional principles, rocked by *Spycatcher*, need to be reaffirmed. Parliament, not the courts, should debate and define the scope of criminal offences. Juries, not judges, should decide whether someone is guilty of a criminal offence. Now, the whole media is at risk of a criminal charge from the Attorney General whenever a confidence injunction has been granted to 'hold the ring'. The existence of this risk has a chilling effect on publication and fosters a self-censorship which is detrimental to the true public interest in a democracy. That risk should be removed by statute.

In Britain there is still no real recognition of the citizens' right to know about the activities of government. Most Western democracies have passed laws entitling citizens to greater access to information. In the courts here, the Government argues that its lawyers should vet and approve what appears in the media; that everything should remain secret unless and until government decides otherwise. These arguments for censorship must be resisted. The law must reassert the right of freedom of speech, which is vital in a democracy and which, as Lord Bridge reminded us, is always the first casualty under a totalitarian regime.

Notes

1.   The English *Spycatcher* cases are reported as *Attorney General* v. *Guardian* at (1987) 1 WLR 1248 (interlocutory injunctions appeals, July 1987) and (1988) 2 WLR 805 (Mr Justice Scott and the Court of Appeal).
2.   The contempt of court action, *Attorney General* v. *Newspaper Publishing* is at (1987) 3 WLR 942.
3.   Prince Albert's etchings are reported in *Albert* v. *Strange* (1849) 1 Mac & G 25.
4.   The Crossman Diaries case, *Attorney General* v. *Jonathan Cape* (1976) QB 752, was followed in Australia by *Commonwealth of Australia* v. *Fairfax* (1980) 147 CLR 39.

12 Whom the Truth Would Indict

Murray Ritchie and Alistair Bonnington

> Here's freedom tae him that wad read
> Here's freedom tae him that wad write
> There's nane ever fear'd that the truth should be heard
> But they whom the truth wad indite.
>
> Robert Burns

On the day it was announced in Parliament that no criminal proceedings would be taken against Duncan Campbell in connection with *Zircon* and the *Secret Society* programmes, the Government switched its attack on freedom of speech by resorting to civil law. The alternative was a criminal prosecution of Campbell in Scotland under Section 2 of the Official Secrets Act, a prospect which filled the hearts of every journalist (except perhaps Mr Campbell) with joy in the confident expectation that there would be not just a resounding acquittal by a Scots jury, but a media event of entertainment value unequalled in the history of music hall.

Mr Campbell had defiantly challenged the Lord Advocate to prosecute him in Scotland for producing the *Secret Society* television series from the BBC studios in Glasgow. Although he had already experienced the trauma of being the accused in a secrets trial (when he was the 'C' in the ABC trial in the 1970s) he was prepared, even willing, to take his chances again. His challenge was never met.

After the abandonment of a criminal case, the Attorney General in England and his opposite number in Scotland, the Lord Advocate, applied to the civil courts for, and obtained, a blanket ban on the reporting of Campbell's revelations about *Zircon* and its role in the gathering of intelligence through GCHQ. The ban applied not just to the BBC but to all television and radio stations and newspapers and magazines in Britain. It also applied not only to information about *Zircon* but to all activities of our secret services.

A blanket ban of this type was quite unprecedented in the very distinct traditions of the Scots legal system. In England such a wide-ranging order was granted to the Government in the *Spycatcher* case but in Scotland the very idea that an interdict (an injunction in England) could apply to all the world was an alien concept in law. In Scots law an interdict was understood to apply only to parties named as defenders and not to any other party with similar interest. Scots law also allows anyone who fears that an interdict might be taken out against them to lodge with the court a *caveat* to prevent an interdict being granted without the defender having an opportunity to appear in court to oppose the application. The effect of this long-standing practice is well established in Scotland. Scottish newspapers, television and radio stations have followed the well worn practice of lodging *caveats*, and have done so for many years as a precaution against some last-minute legal attempt to have them gagged.

In the Campbell case, however, the media was given no opportunity to state its case although the interdict attempted to silence 'any person' having notice of Lord Coulsfield's decision and not just Campbell and the BBC. The reaction in Scotland by journalists and lawyers to this attempted importation of English law was furious and sustained.

Two months later when the Crown sought an interdict on similar terms in the Cavendish memoirs case, the *Glasgow Herald* and Scottish TV took the view that they were not bound by any order taken out against the *Scotsman*. Harry Reid, deputy editor of the *Glasgow Herald*, which had published extracts from Cavendish to support this point of principle in Scots law, said: 'As far as we are concerned the interim interdict did not apply to the *Glasgow Herald* and therefore we cannot have breached it'.

He was supported in this view by one of Scotland's leading legal academics, Professor Robert Black, head of the department of Scots Law at Edinburgh University, who said that the manner of the Government's attempt to prevent the media from reporting disclosures from the memoirs was 'unprecedented'. Professor Black remarked: 'Indeed I would go so far as to say that it goes against the law both in the books and in other cases, inasmuch that in Scotland, hitherto, you could not get an interdict against someone who is not named.'

He accused the Lord Advocate of trying to unify Scots and English law on this critical point: 'That is why he has put in that nasty little phrase [any person] ... I don't think that there is any chance at all that these words just happen to appear there by mistake.' And for good measure he said that while he would not go so far as to say that the Lord Advocate had acted illegally or unconstitutionally he would not baulk at the word 'sinister'.

These developments took place in Scotland in an atmosphere of political reverberation from the *Zircon* case. Not only was the Conservative government of Mrs Thatcher unpopular in Scotland, where only 10 Conservatives had been returned to Parliament from a total of 72 Scottish MPs, but public opinion had been outraged by the appearance of Special Branch police officers at the door of the BBC office in Glasgow. Such a show of force by the secret police in Scotland was quite unprecedented and it attracted huge publicity (not just in Scotland but around the world, notably in the Communist countries of Europe).

The Government seemed to assume that Duncan Campbell was regarded publicly simply as a dissident, left-wing journalist with an obsessive desire to embarrass the Government on security matters. If any such pro-government views were held by the public they were quickly lost when the Lord Advocate applied for new and sweeping authority under the terms of the interdict sought in the Court of Session. Once granted this interdict would have had the effect of silencing not just Duncan Campbell but every print and broadcasting journalist working in Scotland on security subjects.

Lord Coulsfield granted the interim interdict in face of opposition from Campbell's counsel but he refused a request by the Lord Advocate, Lord Cameron of Lochbroom, who did not appear in court, to have the hearing in secret. This was perhaps the first sign that the Scots courts were not willing to be used as a rubber stamp for the Government's policy on official secrecy and even less were they to be taken for granted as an extension of the English legal system.

Duncan Campbell was in the United States when the interim interdict was granted. When he returned he won the backing of the National Union of Journalists for an appeal against Lord Coulsfield's decision. Before an appeal could be lodged, however, other dramatic events unfolded in the Court of Session which meant that Campbell's appeal was put on ice.

The new but related legal wrangle in the Scots secrecy saga arose out of *Inside Intelligence*, a volume of memoirs by Anthony Cavendish, a former MI6 officer who said he had written his book to vindicate the name of his friend, boss and mentor, Sir Maurice Oldfield who, Cavendish felt, had been unfairly treated by Mr Peter Wright, author of *Spycatcher*, and others in their writings on the security services. Cavendish's book had been published, he claimed, for private circulation. He sent about 300 copies to friends as Christmas presents.

In England the *Sunday Times* obtained a copy of Cavendish's memoirs, and on 27 December 1987 they published extracts in a story entitled: 'Secrets of the Old MI6 Man's Christmas Card'. Then on 2 January the Government obtained a blanket ban on any coverage of the book in England. [This ban was subsequently modified to allow some sections to be published. Later (17 January) the *Sunday Times* published articles extracted from the book under the headings 'Wilson was forced to go' and 'Blunders and hostility: how MI5 and MI6 "nobbled" each other in Ulster'.]

There followed a game of cat and mouse between the Scottish media and the courts. In Scotland where the ban had no effect the *Scotsman* reported (5 January) general observations about the book by Mr Tam Dalyell, MP, along with some extracts.

That same day the Lord Advocate, Lord Cameron, sent a telex message to the *Scotsman* asking that the paper immediately give an undertaking not to publish further extracts. Magnus Linklater, the paper's recently-appointed editor, chose not to give this undertaking. That evening a specially-convened late sitting of the Court of Session was asked by the Government to grant a second blanket ban of the type sought successfully in Campbell's case. The judge again was Lord Coulsfield and the judgment again was in favour of the Government, despite the enormous implications it held for the principle of an interdict in Scots law hitherto being applicable only to the party specified in the order.

Lord Coulsfield granted the application with considerable reluctance, making clear that he was doing no more than preserving the Government's position until the implications of the order could be more fully debated. He relied to some extent on the English courts' approach to *Spycatcher* where an order had been sought and obtained against Peter Wright and his publisher, Heinemann, but which had the effect of barring any other writer, publisher or broadcaster from dealing with the same subject.

Next day (6 January) a copy of the book came into the possession of James McKillop, a reporter in the *Glasgow Herald*'s London office. As he was preparing to send extracts to Glasgow for publication, the interdict was served against the *Scotsman* stopping it from using material from the book. After prolonged discussions with his legal advisers, Harry Reid decided to publish the extracts in the following day's issue of the *Glasgow Herald* (7 January). The night before the *Glasgow Herald*'s extracts appeared the *Herald*, *Scotsman* and Scottish Television (STV) lodged a joint appeal against Lord Coulsfield's interdict.

On the evening of 7 January, the *Glasgow Herald* was accused by the Lord Advocate of being in breach of interdict. Its editor, Arnold Kemp, returned from holiday to be met at the door of his office by messengers-at-arms who presented him with a court document telling him that if he were found in breach of interdict he might be imprisoned. 'It was just a grubby little note', Arnold Kemp said later. 'It was difficult to realise that this was the full majesty of the law being brought to bear...' Scottish Television which had also broadcast some of *Inside Intelligence* was also told it was in breach of interdict.

On 18 January the *Scotsman* published an extract, 'How MI5 was brought to book'. Magnus Linklater argued that since the English courts had by now modified their ban to permit Scottish editions of English papers to carry extracts there could be no reason for the Scottish ban being continued. The Lord Advocate also made clear he did not intend pursuing the English papers for breach of interdict.

Lord Coulsfield was now having second thoughts about his judgment. In his written note for the three senior judges who would hear the first of two appeals, he explained that his decision had been made after hearing only sketchy arguments. Having reconsidered the matter at his leisure the judge now took the view that he should not have granted the interdict in the first place. Lord Coulsfield noted that, on the face of it, all of the material in Cavendish's book had already been published elsewhere. He also recognised that the public had an interest in receiving information on security matters from the media as long as national security was not endangered by disclosure.

In this case the Lord Advocate's counsel had categorically conceded that no issue of national security was raised by the distribution of Cavendish's book. In that situation Lord Coulsfield now favoured what he saw as the overriding public interest which was the free exchange of information even about the security services. When the case came to appeal, the Lord Advocate's counsel desperately tried to withdraw this concession by convoluted argument but the bench, on this critical point, proved unyielding.

Indeed the first appeal before the Lord President, Lord Emslie, sitting with the Lords Grieve and Brand, had to be abandoned because the Lord Advocate's counsel had to change tack on the final day, having seen quite clearly that the media was going to win its case. All counsel who addressed the court (including junior Crown counsel) agreed that there was no issue of national security raised by the Cavendish case. However, in the dying hours of the appeal senior counsel for the Crown told the court that national security was indeed involved. The very idea that this late claim could be taken seriously after such impressive agreement among senior and experienced advocates moved their Lordships to make some scathing comments about the Crown's conduct of the case.

They had no hesitation in awarding all costs to the two newspapers and Scottish TV. They went farther and awarded special costs to the media appellants, perhaps as an indication of their impatience with the Crown case. Such a move is unusual in Scots courts procedure and was taken by the *Glasgow Herald*, *Scotsman* and Scottish TV to be a most encouraging sign.

Lord Coulsfield now had the case sent back to him for reappraisal, providing the spectacle, unusual in Scots law, of a judge being required to reconsider his own view taken in reconsideration of his own first judgment. He heard a further six full days of argument that his first judgment was mistaken as he himself had suggested it might be. And so this increasingly farcical legal saga reached the point where Lord Coulsfield, on the bench for only three months and perhaps wishing he had been a bank clerk, was for the second time dealing with the most publicised secrecy case in Scotland after *Zircon*.

In his long judgment he came to the same view as the English Court of Appeal had done on *Spycatcher* – that if the book had been widely publicised then 'the cat was out of the bag' (his words) and there would be no point in granting meaningless court orders to ban publication of material of which the public already had knowledge. Thus he had at last come down on the side of the newspapers and television and against the Lord Advocate and the Government. As the Appeal Court had done before, he awarded costs and special costs against the Crown.

Inevitably, the Government appealed, using its endless supply of taxpayers' money, despite having suffered two ringing defeats in which the demeanour of the Scots judges was notably hostile to the Crown's arguments. This second appeal was heard by Lord Justice-Clerk Ross, Lord Macdonald and Lord Dunpark. Counsel for the Lord Advocate routinely received another pummelling from the hostile Bench.

The three judges found the Lord Advocate's argument on national security unacceptable. They pointed out that he was now asking them to follow the English courts and allow publication of only part of Cavendish's book. (In England the Attorney General and the media had agreed to permit publication of the so-called 'blue-pencilled' version of *Inside Intelligence*, a volume in which offending sections had been obliterated by the Crown.) That request was irreconcilable with his argument that publication of the book (as opposed to its contents) endangered national security.

The Scottish media which, up to this point, had been celebrating its courts' tough and independent line on secrecy law, was chastened by Lord Macdonald's throwaway remark that 'there is no such thing as the freedom of the press'. Lord Macdonald supported this remarkable observation by arguing that the press enjoyed no more freedom in law than the ordinary citizen – although how that denies the existence of freedom of the press is difficult to see except as a legal nicety.

The terms of the three judges' verdict were based on fine points of the law. No longer were there any high-sounding principles involved; the case was reduced to a technical legal argument. The appeal judges ducked basic issues such as free public access to information, freedom of speech and national security and they ignored the fundamental principle of allowing immediate publication of matters of public interest. The case was decided, instead, on the court's view of written arguments submitted by each side.

Yet again the Scottish media had won its case. Yet again it was awarded all costs. But at what price?

Scots judges left the way open for the Crown to appeal to the House of Lords which can consider the decisions of Scots courts in civil but not criminal cases. Paradoxically, if the Crown in Scotland had prosecuted Duncan Campbell and failed to win a conviction, no such appeal would have been competent. By going down the road of civil law the Crown at least earned itself one last chance. At the time of writing the Lords have still to hear the Crown's appeal against the decision of the Scottish judges.

Whichever points of law might be raised by the Lords some fundamental issues have been established by the Scots courts when dealing with secrecy law. By far the most significant is that Scots law refuses to recognise a blanket ban on the media. If government wants to gag a Scottish newspaper or a Scottish television or radio station it must first serve proceedings on the newspaper or broadcast medium involved. If a *caveat* has been lodged by the defenders then they must be given the right to be heard – and that is a process which can take a lot of valuable time in the world of news immediacy.

Interdicts by stealth will not be allowed. In Scotland the Crown will not be permitted to approach the court in secret session at 9.30 am in breach of an understanding reached with the defendant's solicitor; no longer can the Crown obtain an interim order in this way without the defendant having a chance to state his case which is exactly what happened in England to Duncan Campbell.

In Scotland the media will at least have the chance to be heard before a judge. The case will not be heard in secret. These are crucial victories in the resistance to the advance of secrecy law as laid down in recent times by the courts in England and their importance to British law should not be underestimated. The Scottish experience in resisting this systematic and unrelenting assault on the free flow of information, which is fundamental to any sophisticated, Western democracy, should be looked upon as a touchstone for future guidance.

Since the Government began its assault on the British press's challenge to outdated and discredited secrecy laws, a huge financial burden has been placed on individual newspapers and television stations. In the nature of things the newspapers involved are mostly those which are among the least wealthy – in other words the quality press.

For example, in the case of the *Scotsman* and the *Glasgow Herald* the legal fees involved are huge for papers with small circulations (about 100 000 in the case of the *Scotsman* and about 125 00 for the *Herald*) while the principles involved are basic to individual freedom. The Government, using endless supplies of taxpayers' money, is in effect imposing a huge fine on the papers concerned with every stage of litigation. As each stage of the case is resolved to the satisfaction of the media so the costs mount. Although newspapers which win their cases are reportedly awarded costs, the true expense can be astronomical and is never recoverable in full.

It follows that, however important the principle of litigation, the outcome in law can depend on the financial strength of the papers and television stations involved – and not all are equipped for such a long running and expensive battle. There might come a time when financial restraints imposed by purely commercial considerations dictate that the battle for freedom of expression is abandoned.

In other words the Government is seeking to intimidate the media in Britain, with the threat of financial penalties, having begun the process in London and unwittingly stumbled into the minefield of Scots law simply because some bureaucrats in Whitehall had overlooked the fact – if they ever were aware of it – that Scots law was different.

Another more general point now made by many journalists and

lawyers is that the Government, having put publishers, newspapers, television and radio stations through financial hoops, has now made clear that any publication of so-called 'confidential' or 'security' information will be carried out only at the risk of huge cost.

Heinemann's lawyer says that the publishing house has spent more than £1m so far on defending *Spycatcher* and not all of that will be recoverable. Reputedly, the costs met by the *Observer* so far are more than £1m. The same will apply to the *Sunday Times* and the *Guardian* (which is run by a trust). If the Government were to fail in its inexorable pursuit of the press and television through every court in the land, and yet impose such huge costs on the media, who then will publish another *Spycatcher* or *Inside Intelligence* and be damned to financial ruin?

13 Government and Secrecy – Parliament's Search for Truth

Nigel Spearing

Whatever the political difference between the parties in the high profile Parliament of 1974–79, one thing was agreed: the need to assert the right of Parliament to know more of what the Whitehall machine was up to; and to penetrate unjustifiable curtains of confidentiality in the cause of both efficiency and accountability.

Since then the issue has become even more urgent. We have a Government which, despite its public pronouncements, has centralised power in Whitehall still further, and has so structured itself around the personality of the Prime Minister, that each of the interlocking organs of the Executive has become autocratic too. It is ironic that 300 years after the 'Glorious Revolution', when Parliament asserted its sovereignty over personalised autocracy, we now have a Government that is again rolling forward the frontiers of arbitrary power (incidentally in the name of rolling back the frontiers of the state!). At the same time Parliament appears unable properly to detect and expose the hidden operation of that arbitrary power.

The failure may be partly explained by the essentially hierarchical and secretive manner in which Whitehall operates. The Palace of Whitehall may have been demolished but behind the scenes court-style politics persist. There has thus been even more conflict along the permanently changing frontier between open opinion, information and debate in the public realm and that which is subject to secrecy. While confidentiality and secrecy is held to be necessary 'in the public interest' it also serves to mask both the irresponsible use of power and the internecine conflict which the Thatcher style of government inevitably promotes. How can Parliament both check abuse and determine where the frontier should be drawn?

In performing its role of scrutiny of the Executive, Parliament and its individual Members have a wide variety of tools to hand. They can question ministers by letter, at Question Time and in debate. But with the investigatory Select Committees it is their *corporate* power and activities which matter. This is partly because on many issues they eliminate party differences, but also in 'grand confrontation' they mark that frontier between the '*glasnost*' of the public realm and that which governments wish to keep secret – for good or ill.

Acceding to the universal desire to give Parliament better means of investigation, the Labour Government of 1976 established a Select Committee on Procedure, which produced a package of measures designed to weight the scales in Parliament's favour. The best known innovation was the establishment for the first time of a comprehensive pattern of Departmental Select Committees, each charged with the responsibility of shadowing its respective Department and Cabinet member by using all the customary powers of the long established Select Committee Procedure.

It was through the efforts of successive Leaders of the House, Ted Short, Frances Pym and Norman St John-Stevas, that these new Select Committees replaced the less coherent pattern of the *ad hoc* and Expenditure Committees that had previously attempted that role. It was hoped that by using their extensive powers when questioning Cabinet Ministers and senior civil servants in public, their investigations would roll back frontiers of secrecy that had extended far too far.

Success would not be automatic, or indeed easy. MPs have manifold responsibilities, and these are increasing year by year. Thus the sheer difficulty of being able to concentrate on a single issue, which of itself might be multi-faceted, is highly demanding, even with the assistance of experienced Clerks of the House and specialist advisers.

However, the potential is considerable. The process is itself essentially forensic; unlike Question Time when individual questions cannot be properly pursued, there is the opportunity to question the powerful at length, often with expert outside advice, with Memoranda from Departments, and addressing issues chosen by the Committee. Where things have gone wrong a Committee may attempt to find out the real 'plot' from reluctant Government witnesses. There may not be a dead body, but when the chase is on effective Committee members can be as assiduous as detectives in attempting to obtain the truth from willing and unwilling witnesses alike – and ending up with a verdict which rings true on the evidence provided. It is this latter quality which distinguishes their work from the more familiar debating mode of the House. It is often more akin to a court. Exposure of the party political hurly burly, essential though it be, can sometimes obscure the many fundamental constitutional functions which Parliament must fulfil as part of its sovereign authority.

For those Committee members whose party adherence is to the government of the day, coming to a Conclusion which may be unwelcome to that government can be a problem. Since the Committee's Conclusion must be based on the evidence, its language must be measured. This may not be good news for headline writers but it does provide references to the evidence and opportunities for comment or criticism, which otherwise might not emerge. Opposition Members will of course wish to publicise the *proven* warts. But they may be willing to accept less trenchantly expressed Conclusions in order to furnish a Report with the political punch of unanimity.

When party political considerations are absent, the task is easier. When they are present the task of Report making is more delicate. The greatest problems occur when matters of probity are concerned, on which the political life of a minister, or even a government, might depend. In such cases the dilemmas for government supporters become acute. But Parliament set up these watchdog committees to detect abuse of power; when it is detected the duty of government supporters must be to Parliament first. If the evidence is clear and the needs of democratic accountability prevail then an agreed and often strongly critical Report can result. When this happens, as in the Westland case, it must be taken very seriously indeed.

After all, those opposed to the government, or the terms of the draft Report can produce a 'minority' Report. Where this occurs it is still highly significant since all the Conclusions and comment stem from the same evidence. This did in fact occur in the Foreign Affairs Committee Report into the events of the 1–2 May 1982 when Government action came under scrutiny over the sinking of the *Belgrano*.

The importance of the Westland and Falkland Reports however is much greater than merely illustrating the widest alternative options open to Members. Separately and together they raise issues central to the workings of Departmental Committees. Each involved the Prime Minister as the central character; each raised the issue of 'justified or unjustified secrecy'; each raised the 'conscience' issue for senior civil servants (the Falkland issue provoking the Ponting trial and acquittal); and each raised the question of the internal coherence of the policy and actions of the Government.

It is little wonder that the Westland Report[1] was both devastatingly critical and unanimous. The civil war within Whitehall had already reached epic proportions and had spilled into the media well before the dramatic resignation from the Cabinet of the Secretary of State for Defence, Michael Heseltine. His walkout from the Cabinet meeting on 9 January 1986 and his later accusations against the Prime Minister of doctoring Cabinet minutes surely has no parallel in modern times.

Less dramatic, but ultimately of even more crucial importance, was the leak of some of the contents of a confidential letter sent to him on Monday 6 January by the Solicitor General, the government's legal adviser.[2] At first it was assumed that this leak was one of a 'lower deck' series already plaguing Whitehall. Far from it: it turned out to have been authorised by none other than the Secretary of State for Trade and Industry, Leon Brittan. (After bitter controversy in a re-assembled House of Commons he too resigned on 24 January.) The Prime Minister was suspected of being behind the whole affair since it was she who, from all the evidence, appeared to have initiated the request to the Solicitor General and supported Brittan's action in authorising the disclosure. Subsequently on 27 January she too faced a critical debate in the House of Commons, initiated by the Opposition. She survived the debate but later commented that she had not known if she would still be Prime Minister after six o'clock that evening.

It is as well to recall the background to all these extraordinary events. Two major groups, the huge American United Technologies–Sikorsky combine and a European consortium, were competing for the Westland Helicopter Company. The official Government line was simply that this was a matter for the Board and shareholders of the Company to decide. Behind this façade two feuding camps were well established in the Cabinet. The Prime Minister favoured the Sikorsky deal, Michael Heseltine the European. Despite Westland's importance for the Ministry of Defence as the only British helicopter manufacturer, the sponsoring government department was Trade and Industry, headed by Brittan.

As well as taking their war into the media the rival companies were outbidding each other in buying shares in Westland, whose share values were soaring way above their real worth.

At the same time, within a government obsessed with its own secrecy, and partly indeed because of that, yet another curious war of leak and counter leak was now taking place. On Friday 3 January Heseltine sent a letter to the principal backers of the European consortium, Lloyds Merchant Bank. (In reply to a letter his Department had already solicited from them!) His intention was quite clear: it was used to influence the decision of the Westland shareholders in the direction of the European bid and against the Prime Minister and Brittan's view. In the words of the subsequent Westland Report:

> It is clear that this letter was solicited by officials of the Ministry of Defence as a device for making public the material which had been suggested for inclusion in the Prime Minister's [earlier] reply to Sir John Cuckney [Chairman of Westlands] which had been rejected. [by No 10.]

It was known that Cuckney was to give an important press conference on Monday 6 January at 4 pm, when the relative merits of the rival offers would be the agenda. And so too would official information relating to it, including the contents of the Prime Minister's letter. Hence Heseltine's letter to Lloyds, restoring his arguments cut from the Prime Minister's letter.

Since that letter was not cleared with either the Prime Minister or Brittan and was addressed to the chief backer of the European consortium, rather than to the Chairman of Westland, there would be little time for an effective rejoinder. The effect on the Prime Minister, in the words of the Westland Committee,

> can have been nothing short of incendiary. Material which three days before had been excluded from the Prime Minister's letter had been sent, by a crude device . . ., to the European Consortium.

The Prime Minister, keen for once that all the material facts entered the public realm, then engineered[3] a letter from the Solicitor General to Heseltine commenting on Heseltine's letter to Lloyds. As the Solicitor General relied on a text published in *The Times* and on documentation in his office he carefully stated that his opinion was based only on documents he had seen so far ('which I emphasise are all that I have seen.')

Unknown to Downing Street, Heseltine had assured the Solicitor General on the telephone that he possessed documents to back up his claims. A copy of the Solicitor General's letter to Heseltine was delivered to the Department of Trade and Industry about 1 pm on Monday 6 January, where, according to the Select Committee, 'officials had in mind that some public use of the information contained in the letter was indicated.' Brittan agreed that it 'should go into the public domain and that it should be done in specific terms but that No. 10, the Prime Minister's Office, should be consulted.' The final result was that the No. 10 Press Office entrusted the DTI to leak the letter's contents to the Press Association. This was done on an 'unattributable' basis.

This extraordinary situation of Cabinet Ministers and senior officials conniving in this way and using a press agency in order to destroy a fellow Cabinet member and establish Government policy stems directly from the secrecy of British governmental structures, and even more importantly from the consequent exploitation of that secrecy, both by civil servants and their ministers.

The effect of this secrecy is compounded by the inadequacies of the Parliamentary Question Time structure which prevents the pursuit of truth through forensic methods and allows any skilful minister to avoid the admission of accountability. In this case it enabled the Prime Minister to make apparently contradictory statements about her responsibility in the matter of the leaked letter, a question which has never been finally and absolutely answered. The record of the House is striking:

> Prime Minister: It was to get that accurate information to the public domain that I gave my consent. (*Hansard* 23 January 1986)
> Prime Minister: I did not give my consent to the disclosure. It was not sought and I have indicated that I deeply regret the manner in which it was made. (*Hansard* 27 January 1986)

(This contradiction was later defended by Sir Robert Armstrong, Cabinet Secretary, as 'a slip of the tongue'. (Westland Report Question 1252))

However, whether she regretted it or not, this had one inestimable advantage to No. 10, which the Select Committee pointed out in classic and cutting terms: 'The objective of unattributable disclosure of information is to seek to influence without accepting responsibility.' (Westland Report, paragraph 168)

How is it that with a Report like this, coupled with the doubts already raised in the debate in the House of Commons on 27 January, the Government could survive? The short answer is that at the time of that crucial debate fewer facts were provable. Heseltine had resigned. Brittan had just been sacrificed. After that, the vested interests in the survival of the Government were greater than the forces conscious of the necessity for accountable, representative government.

A second factor is the changing values in news, now a daily commodity. Despite its real importance the trenchant Committee Report made little impact, although the evidence was devastating and revealed a state of Government conduct which would have resulted in the fall of a Prime Minister in most democracies.

Partly it was the nature of British Select Committees. For whatever reason, they chose not to invite those senior civil servants most directly involved (such as Bernard Ingham and Colette Bowe) to appear before them – nor the Prime Minister. Sir Robert Armstrong, however, *did* appear. Leon Brittan appeared but, unlike the situation in the USA, because he was not required to answer questions, chose not to where it really mattered.

Indeed at one point Dr John Gilbert said: 'I would like to get a list of questions you are not prepared to answer.' And over several subsequent columns Brittan refused to answer any questions relating to the leak. It might have been good slapstick but not very informative – however illuminating!

Disturbingly, the Government's response was not that we should have more open government but how they could impose a greater secrecy. They decided to block any future possibility of a senior civil servant giving evidence on the 'conduct' of other named civil servants. In their reply to the Westland Report the Government said:

> Accordingly the Government proposes to make it clear to civil servants giving evidence to Select Committees that they should not answer questions which are or appear to be directed to the conduct of themselves or of other named individual civil servants.[4]

It was a brutal declaration of the supremacy of government over parliament. It set the alarm bells ringing in the House of Commons, particularly among Select Committee Chairmen. It is typical in the war of constitutional propriety and in defence of accountable and representative government that authoritarianism will advance by means of small print. The Treasury and Civil Service Select Committee found the reply inflammatory, if not, indeed, incendiary. They were already conducting an enquiry into the accountability of civil servants. Revealingly the Government was replying to a Treasury and Civil Service Report on this very topic on the same day as they had replied to the Westland Report. However, revealingly or arrogantly, they made this new policy statement in reply to the Westland Committee and not to the Treasury and Civil Service Committee, showing that it was in fact a response to their near bruising over Westland. Not surprisingly this created even more irritation.

The Civil Service Committee answered back:

We are in no doubt that it would be quite wrong and entirely unacceptable for any restrictions to be placed on the giving of such evidence and we are sure that on reflection the Government have no intention of doing any such thing. It is obviously highly desirable that the Government should make this clear.

The Government resisted this and it required a meeting of all the Chairmen of the Select Committees to issue a recommendation 'that the proposed government instruction should not be issued' before the Government agreed to amend their proposals.

Nevertheless the fact that the two senior Select Committees had to make this amount of effort to stem both the advancing tide of secrecy and to thwart attempts to undermine the effectiveness of Select Committees is of great constitutional significance. The challenge to the sovereignty of the House demonstrates the continuing encroachment of autocracy.

Representative government demands the sovereignty of public representatives – in our case the House of Commons. The Executive should satisfy both Parliament and people that it is operating efficiently and with probity and coherence, that publicly declared policies are followed and that words and actions of ministers are consistent, and seen to be so.

Where secrecy and confidentiality are necessary, and there will be different views about where the line should be drawn, representatives of Parliament are entitled to be assured that the claimed coherence and probity do in fact exist – hence the demands for a Select Committee in the field of security, composed of Privy Councillors.

Security considerations have been too often used by government as an excuse for not divulging information that would bear witness to the inconsistency of the official story. Clive Ponting divulged information to Tam Dalyell because the official line, whilst possibly consistent within itself, was not consistent with the truth. The fear of a 'breach in our united front'[5] was the reason why the Ministry of Defence attempted to hide information from the Foreign Affairs Committee over changes to 'Rules of Engagement' in the Falklands conflict.

In the Westland affair the 'united front' of the Prime Minister was the overriding need to get information into the public realm! The twin scandals of Falklands and Westland illustrate the degree to which the Select Committees mark the frontier war between democracy and autocracy.

No doubt there will be demands for an assessment of how successful these Select Committees have been. An understandable desire but to an extent misplaced. Each should be judged on its own merits and on its own Reports. But the overriding question should be 'how stands the frontier between Executive and Parliament – how far has the veil of secrecy been used to cloak unaccountable activities of the Executive?' The facts surely show that despite the existence of the Committees the frontiers are still moving against Parliament. Ironically, three centuries after the Glorious Revolution we are seeing the re-emergence of a kind of *de facto*, arbitrary and authoritarian power.

One answer must lie in the strengthening of these Select Committees. Their activities must be given greater prominence in the media and greater attention by Parliament and commentators. The Committees themselves must be given more powers in exercising their right to investigate, question and be answered. Otherwise our ancient liberties, won mainly by the use of word, pen and tongue will be at risk. Indeed, some would say, they are already.

Notes

1. Fourth Report from the Defence Committee Session 1985–86 Westland plc: The Government's Decision-Making (HC 519)
2. The senior legal adviser to the government is the Attorney General, who was abroad at the time. Legal officers' advice is always regarded as highly confidential throughout government.
3. Paragraph 134 of Fourth Report from the Defence Committee Session 1985–86 Westland plc: The Government's Decision-Making (HC 519).
4. Westland plc: The Defence Implications of the Future of Westland plc: The Government's decision-making – Government Response to the Third and Fourth Reports from the Defence Committee, Session 1985–86, HC518 and 519 (Cmnd. 9916).
5. Third Report from the Foreign Affairs Committee Session 1984–85 Events Surrounding the Weekend of 1–2 May 1982 (HC11) Page cxiii Paragraph 7.30 of The Minority Report.

14 What Price the Arts?
Michael Billington

Matthew Arnold, I suspect, is not much read nowadays, but he had the right idea. In 1869 he published a lecture, *Sweetness and Light*, which included the following passage:

> It [culture] does not try to reach down to the level of inferior classes; it does not try to win them for this or that sect of its own with ready-made judgements and watchwords. It seeks to do away with classes; to make the best that has been thought and known in the world current everywhere; to make all men live in an atmosphere of sweetness and light where they may use ideas freely, nourished and not bound by them.

A decade later he wrote an essay, *The French Play in London*, which welcomed the arrival of the Comédie Française in London and which contrasted their tradition, esteem and high degree of organisation with the merciless chaos of the English theatre: 'We gladly took refuge in our favourite doctrines of the mischief of State interference, of the blessedness of leaving every man to do as he likes, of the impertinence of presuming to check any man's natural taste for the bathos and pressing him to relish the sublime. We left the English theatre to take its chance. Its present impotence is the result.'

Matthew Arnold's words have a melancholy ring today. The post-war consensus that the arts are everyone's entitlement and the responsibility of government, national and local, to provide is rapidly being eroded. The complex network of subsidy is being dismantled bit by bit. What we are witnessing is a gradual shift from state-funding to private sponsorship which brings in its wake hidden censorship, dilution of quality and, along with that, a bland acceptability as a criterion of judgement. The Arts Council, long regarded as a model example of how to distribute subsidy without strings, has been transformed under Sir William (now Lord) Rees-Mogg into a tool of government: its cheeseparing funds now come loaded with all kinds of conditions and *caveats*. On top of that the government, through Section 28 of the Local Government Act and its attempt to stifle works that promote homosexuality, has blatantly re-introduced official censorship of the arts 20 years after the abolition of the Lord Chamberlain's arbitrary theatrical powers. Not even the Thatcher government has the courage to cut off all funding to the arts (which is the ultimate logic of its *laisser-faire* beliefs). Instead it is doing something more insidious: using economic deprivation as a means of keeping the arts under control. The only hope is that it can never entirely succeed because of the artist's own instinctively subversive tendencies.

Our attitude to the arts in Britain has always been somewhat equivocal. We want them; but we don't much like paying for them. The great breakthrough, however, came during the last war with the creation of the Committee for the Encouragement of Music and the Arts (CEMA) which established the principle of government subsidy. In 1945 that became the Arts Council with Maynard Keynes as its first Chairman. As Bryan Appleyard wrote in *The Culture Club*: 'It was part of a package which included the National Health Service, national insurance, nationalised industries and free orange juice – all of them practical, pragmatic, centralised ways to a better future.' The tap of subsidy wasn't exactly gushing but at least it was connected; and the Arts Council itself operated in a personal, beneficent manner. In the early 1960s I worked for a theatre company based in Lincoln that toured every month to Rotherham, Loughborough and Scunthorpe. I well remember how the Arts Council's Drama Director, Joe Hodgkinson, used to pay us regular visits to discuss our constant financial problems. But in those enlightened, far-off days the subsidy was determined by the quality of the work and its touring availability rather than by bottoms-on-seats or our ability to attract outside patronage. The fact that we were offering a diet of Shakespeare, Congreve, Arden and Pinter to audiences spread over three counties was thought to be sufficient to warrant a decent subsidy.

Since then the Arts Council has grown enormously in scale; Regional Arts Associations have sprung up all over the country; the late 1960s and early 1970s saw an enormous boom in the development of new theatres, galleries, concert-halls and multi-purpose arts centres as well as a proliferation of small-scale ventures roughly categorised as the Fringe. All this led to a heady feeling that the arts in Britain were no longer doomed to be in the exclusive preserve of a small, middle-class minority but were at last coming within the reach, both financially and geographically, of anyone who wanted them. The arts even vaulted into the larger economic arena. Bryan Appleyard estimated in 1984 that, without broadcasting and publishing, the arts industry had an estimated turnover of £1000 million.

Even William Rees-Mogg was moved to point out that the arts were a good investment and that the government received back, in a variety of ways, 75 per cent of its initial expenditure.

None of this seems to have impressed Mrs Thatcher. What has happened during her period in office is not merely a succession of annual cutbacks to the arts but a profound change in philosophy. She clearly believes that if the arts are any good, they must stand on their own two feet; and that, if they need patronage, they must look less to central and local government and more to private and corporate sponsorship as in the United States (without, however, any change in the tax laws to act as an incentive to business sponsorship). Mrs Thatcher's first Arts Minister, Norman St John-Stevas, argued that the policy of rolling back the frontiers of the state could have 'no logical application to the arts'. In contrast her current Arts Minister, Richard Luce, in 1987 told a convention of arts administrators that 'the only real test of our ability to succeed is whether or not we can attract enough customers.' The *only* test? By that vulgar criterion, the plays of Harold Pinter, the operas of Benjamin Britten, the symphonies of Michael Tippett, the paintings of Lucian Freud would have been strangled at birth. By that criterion, Andrew Lloyd Webber is a greater composer than Sir Harrison Birtwhistle, Ray Cooney is a greater dramatist than John Osborne and Tretchikoff is the ultimate modern artist.

We live in a society where commerce is the prime criterion of artistic value. My contention is that this amounts to censorship, that it shows a profound ignorance of the possibilities of artistic growth and that, even in its own market-place terms, it is criminally silly since our identity as a nation is tied up with the quality and variety of our subsidised art.

I can speak best of the theatre – it is my daily work. What I have witnessed over the last decade is not some sudden apocalyptic crisis but a steady, subversive dilution of values; a lessening of quality; an all too ready acceptance of the idea that 'Thatcherism has re-set the agenda'.

Let me take a specific area: classic theatre. It seems to me part of every person's right to have available the great works of the past, both native and foreign, wherever they may live. No one is forced to go to them; but they should be easily accessible. I grew up in the Midlands and carried out much of my own theatrical education at Sir Barry Jackson's Birmingham Rep in the late 1950s and early 1960s. In that era I was able to see – at ludicrously cheap prices – not only a wealth of Shakespeare but Restoration and 18th century comedy, Greek, French and Italian classic drama (the Germans, as usual, never got much of a look in). Birmingham now has a handsome, plate-glass repertory theatre with a main auditorium and a studio; but, like most theatres of its kind, it has to exist on a diet of reasonably popular choices with risk pared to a minimum. The hunger for classics is still there (a studio Shakespeare season by the Renaissance Theatre Company was packed to the rafters); but large-scale productions of large-cast plays have now become economically impossible.

I am not making this up. In 1986 I was a member of Sir Kenneth Cork's Enquiry team that looked at the state of professional theatre in England. Our report included a statistical table analysing the repertoire at Arts Council-funded regional theatres over a 14-year period. In 1974 classics (generously defined as pre-war, non-Shakespearean drama) amounted to 22 per cent of the repertory. By 1979 the figure was down to 15 per cent. By 1984 it was down to 8 per cent. The reason is simple: money. It has now become dauntingly expensive to mount any play with a cast of more than ten. In practice, that means that main-house Shakespeare and the whole classic tradition is in danger of going down the chute.

Does it matter? I believe passionately that it does. It means that a whole generation is growing up that will never have been exposed to classic drama in all its richness. It also means that actors, directors, designers are getting fewer and fewer chances to stretch their muscles in the great classic plays, Shakespeare included. The consequences of this are slowly becoming visible. It means that actors are now stepping out on to the large stage of the Royal Shakespeare Theatre in Stratford upon Avon hopelessly ill-equipped to speak Shakespeare's verse. It also means – as Richard Eyre's production of *The Changeling* at the National recently proved – that actors lack the vocal and technical resources to cope with Jacobean drama. It may seem a long way from Thatcher's self-help policies to the decline in English verse-speaking. In fact, it is not. Less money means smaller casts. Smaller casts mean fewer classics. Fewer classics mean less opportunity to tangle with the complexities of the great masterpieces. The choices are all the time becoming narrower; and that, in itself, is a form of censorship.

Even the great classic companies are being undermined by the prevailing commercial ethos. The Royal Shakespeare Company was created in 1960 by Peter Hall both to establish the importance of permanence and continuity and to link the Shakespearean and the modern tradition: in the late 1980s the Company has now become famous, and even notorious, as a purveyor of musicals. And once again the reasons are primarily economic. In 1983 the Thatcher Government set up the Priestley Report into 'The Financial Affairs and Financial Prospects of the Royal Opera House, Covent Garden and the Royal Shakespeare Company'. The hope was clearly that civil service scrutiny would confirm vague impressions of waste and extravagance and lead the way to swingeing cuts. In fact, the Priestley Report was a considerable embarrassment to the government: it proved that both organisations were, by and large, well-run and badly underfunded. In the short term, the RSC got an immediate hike in its grant: in the long term it has been given the usual niggling grant-increases which, after inflation, amount to annual cuts.

The result is that the RSC has had to sell its soul for a mess of musicals. It went into partnership with a commercial management to produce *Les Misérables*, profits from which around the world are currently helping to keep the company afloat. Since then it has staged *Kiss Me Kate*, *The Wizard of Oz* and the disastrous *Carrie* which recently lost more money (though not the British taxpayers') than any other production in New York history. But *Carrie* is the ultimate logic of Thatcherite economics. A once great classic company is forced to do commercial deals and stage a piece of cynical youth-market trash which then doesn't even succeed in the market-place. This is what we have been reduced to in the current climate.

But the RSC, in another way, also offers a chilling example of what can happen to a once-legendary institution under Thatcherism. In 1987 the company was in dire financial straits. Technically, it was bankrupt. The only solution seemed to be to close down either the Stratford or the London end of its operations. In the end, it was saved from the brink by a sponsorship deal with Royal Insurance who offered to put a million pounds into the company over a three-year period. But sponsors are not fools. They want something in return for their money. What Royal Insurance have is priority billing (far above that given to the Arts Council) on all RSC programmes, leaflets, brochures and notepaper. They also asked that the RSC tour to major cities where the Royal Insurance Company is based. This led to a nightmarish scheduling at Stratford in 1988 and the creation of a company-within-a-company capable of being detached and sent out on the road.

The point is that sponsorship is implicit censorship. It is a means of dictating what gets done. Public subsidy comes with the understanding – or at least it always has in the past – that the beneficiary has the right to determine how the money is spent: if it is flagrantly mis-used or the product is bad, then it can always be withdrawn. But sponsorship clearly comes with strings attached. It favours the safe, the established, the unchallenging. It is not that difficult to get sponsorship for a subscription season of symphony concerts, for a classical ballet, for a nineteenth-century opera, for Shakespeare; but try getting it for a Howard Brenton season at the Royal Court! Even classical productions have to have the right sound, as the National Theatre discovered to its cost when its production of *'Tis Pity She's a Whore* was felt not to have the right image-boosting quality by any of Britain's major corporations.

Sir Peter Hall has spoken of 'the corruption of sponsorship'. He is right. It is corrupting in that it favours certain types of art over others and inevitably leads to a form of self-censorship. It also leads to a form of greedy self-aggrandisement on the part of the money-men. Travelling back from Tbilisi where I had been watching the National Theatre stage three late Shakespeare plays, I was accosted by a businessman who told me that his firm had sponsored the trip: no mention of the fact that it was the British Council's £100 000 which in fact had enabled the NT to travel to the Soviet Union in the first place.

Sponsorship is given with strings and can be arbitrarily withdrawn. It is also no more than a topping-up operation: even the Royal Opera House, with its enormous prestige, gets no more than seven per cent of its total revenue from this source. For most companies – outside the big four national drama and opera companies – it is a total waste of time. One theatre director told me that he used to flog round local companies trying to raise moneys to match the play, going to Bryant and May's for instance to support *The Matchmaker*: that is not what theatre directors are for. An administrator at Leeds Playhouse also told me that the amount of money generated by sponsorship failed to match the salary of the person hired to tout round local industries.

It is nonsense for the government to pretend that corporate patronage can ever take the burden off the state to fund the arts. But it is worse than nonsense. It is a way of softening the product, limiting the choices available and handing over artistic authority to board-room figures ill-equipped to handle it.

What worries me, in general, is that arts funding in Britain is gradually ceasing to be a form of disinterested benefaction and becoming more and more a means of exercising control. Richard

Luce, in person, is a perfectly amiable man but I was shocked to find him reported as saying in 1987 that people who kept on attacking the Government (and he clearly had Sir Peter Hall in mind) were jeopardising their own chances of increased subsidy: in other words, silence was now becoming the price for subvention. The Arts Council's attitude to its clients is also subtly changing: a totally apolitical new-writing company like Paines Plough gets a huge increase in grant while directly political groups like Foco Novo or 7:84 get either swingeing cuts or the complete severance of life-support subsidies. The whole system of incentive-funding which the Arts Council is currently devising also means that extra funds will go not to those who are artistically adventurous but to those companies who can raise private money for capital development schemes. We used to reward people for doing plays: we now reward them for their entrepreneurial skill in handling real estate.

But I am sorry to say that the policy of treating arts funding as some kind of political football is not confined to the Right. I was saddened recently to find Greater London Arts threatening to cut their grant to the Almeida in Islington by 12 per cent on the grounds that the audience was insufficiently multi-racial and that the Almeida did not give the highest priority to black arts and multi-racial casting. With Maya Angelou about to direct Errol John's *Moon on a Rainbow Shawl* the timing was singularly maladroit. It also struck me as a heavy-handed way of making a political point. Of course, multi-racial casting and audience-composition is vital; but consultation and discussion are more likely to achieve it than brandishing subsidy-cuts as a form of moral pressure. Once again one found the arm's-length principle of subsidy, which used to be an article of faith, being replaced by the strong-arm method with subvention used as a lever of power.

Local authorities, subject to rate-capping, have also occasionally used withdrawal of arts funds as a political weapon. I am never quite sure how much this is a calculated tactic to galvanise the middle classes and how much it amounts to a real threat. But in 1987 we found Hammersmith and Fulham Council, which had previously been stalwart in its support of the Lyric Hammersmith, suddenly threatening to withdraw funds completely unless the theatre launched a more popular programme. No one of course ever defines what 'popular' means: I suspect the Council didn't mean Goethe's *Faust*, which went on both to earn laudatory reviews and to fill seats for a long run. But once again it seemed to me dubious to throw a year's work into disarray in order to get across the point that the Council was being penalised by the government.

But it is the Thatcher government which has done most to stifle debate by keeping the theatre on short commons. In the end, of course, you never can totally silence the artist and reports of the death of political theatre strike me as greatly exaggerated: plays like Caryl Churchill's *Serious Money*, Tony Marchant's *Speculators*, Howard Brenton's *Greenland* have shown that there is still plenty of mileage to be got out of attacking the greed, rapacity, cruelty and intransigent egotism of the era through which we are living. Modern drama has not been silenced. It has, however, been circumscribed. Quite simply, it is getting harder and harder to finance big public plays written on a large and generous scale: a work like David Edgar's *Maydays* which analysed the failure of the post-war socialist dream would find it very difficult to get a production in the late 1980s. Dramatists these days either seem to be writing on a more modest, intimate scale or using the past as a metaphor for the present.

Censorship takes many forms. It can be economic, as with the slow erosion of public money to the arts. It can be hidden, as with the reversal to private sponsorship which instantly precludes certain types of art. It can be frontal, as in the case of Section 28 which, if interpreted literally, could mean books being banned from libraries, pictures taken off gallery walls and plays by writers from Marlowe to Tennessee Williams being prevented from being seen on public stages. It is not merely a monstrous foolish piece of legislation. It is the thin end of a dangerous wedge which threatens all our liberties and means that someone in authority has the power to dictate what we shall read, hear and see.

But what finally troubles me about the arts in Britain today is that we are all getting used to settling for less. We are getting into a state where we take it as axiomatic that classical companies will mount gaudy musicals, that the Royal Court will stage no more than four major productions a year, that major exhibitions will come with the name of the sponsor blazoned as large as that of the gallery or the artist, that the English National Opera's (ENO) Administrator will come before the curtain nightly appealing for funds, that cinema and television will be governed by a promiscuous nostalgia for some lost golden age. The worst affliction of our age is a kind of spiritual *ennui* stemming from a belief that it is impossible to change anything.

The arts in Britain have been damaged but not eroded. I think it is important that we still go on protesting every time a Fringe company is cut, every time a building is closed, every time a local initiative is stifled. I also think it is vital that artists carry the battle into the enemy camp and continue to attack the denial of basic freedoms, the elevation of greed into a national principle, the circulation of lies as if they were fundamental truths. The evidence is that when artists – like Caryl Churchill in the theatre, Hanif Kureishi in the cinema or Charles Wood on television – do attack the spirit of the age they find a ready response. Art should be constantly vigilant against tyranny: and in these dark times, when the Thought Police are abroad, it is a prime function of the creative spirit to register eloquent protest.

15 Danger in the Wings
Phyllida Shaw

Extract from National Campaign for the Arts News (Spring 1988)

Mr Luce has marketed sponsorship well to his parliamentary colleagues, but theatres are not so certain that it is a good thing. Theatre is, after festivals and music, the third most popular art form among sponsors and in 1986–7 it earned 15 per cent of the one and three quarter million pounds provided by the Government under the Business Sponsorship Incentive Scheme (Source: *Hansard*, Col.507, 1 March 1988). A large amount of money though this may seem, individually threatres do not benefit greatly from sponsorship. It is still very much the 'icing on the cake'. Of the theatres we surveyed, not one of them has attracted more than 6 per cent of its income through sponsorship and most considerably less (See table 15.1).

The relative wealth of the region, the type of audience catered to and the appeal of a theatre's work to a potential sponsor, make for great variations in the amount of sponsorship a theatre can attract. There are examples of successful sponsorship deals, which benefit sponsor and theatre alike, such as Mobil's playwright competition at the Royal Exchange, Manchester and BP's Young Directors' Festival at Battersea Arts Centre, but for every successful attempt, there are hundreds of abandoned ones. The level of disappointment on the part of theatres relates directly to the cost in terms of time, skill and money which they have to devote to pursuing sponsors.

Even when you can afford a professional fundraiser, as the Theatre Royal, Stratford East discovered, it is no simple matter to change a sponsor's perceptions of an area, the likely targetability of the audience and the appeal of the artistic programme. The Theatre Royal, which was started by Joan Littlewood in one of the poorest boroughs in the country, and which is known, appropriately, as Pioneer Theatres Ltd, abandoned the search for sponsorship in 1984, having paid a fundraiser for three years without even managing to raise his salary. Even having won the *Daily Telegraph*'s first annual award for the best use of sponsorship money did not seem to be an attraction. The Liverpool Everyman confirms the experience: 'We spend much more time on sponsorship and other private contributions

Table 15.1   Percentage of income from public and private sources

Theatre	Public[1]	Box Office	Sponsors	Other[2]
Bush Theatre, London	74	23	0.0	2.5
Colchester, Mercury	40	53	0.5	6.7
Coventry, Belgrade	65	26	0.2	8.7
Derby, Playhouse	50	37	1.3	7.4
Edinburgh, Traverse	59	22.6	5.8	12.1
Glasgow, Citizens'	62	30	0.8	6.5
Hammersmith, Lyric	49	39	1.1	10.5
Leeds, Playhouse	57	35	0.3	7.5
Liverpool, Everyman	66	20.6	3.7	9.9
Liverpool, Playhouse	66	23	5.3	5.6
Norwich, Theatre Royal	0.3	86	0.2	13.1
Oldham, Coliseum	55	36	0.4	7.8
Plymouth, Theatre Royal	34	43	0.0	23.0
Theatre Royal, Stratford East	74	22	0.0	3.8

[1] Arts Council, RAA and local authority funding combined
[2] Other includes sales, restaurant, investment income, donations, and transfers

Source: National Campaign for the Arts Survey February 1988

and much less on internal financial and other controls. It is questionable whether the change has been cost effective.'

The Bush, a fringe theatre in west London, illustrates other hurdles. Fringe theatres have a tradition of lower priced tickets and with fewer than 100 seats, there is a limit to the amount of income the Bush can raise from the audience. Sponsorship might seem an obvious alternative source of income. 'Unfortunately, commercial sponsorship for an organisation such as our own is not feasible, for several reasons, such as our size, the time which we can devote to sponsorship and the political content of some of our productions.' Sponsors prefer larger audiences and uncontroversial work. Last summer there was a fire at the theatre. Individuals have given £25 000 towards the refurbishment. Private companies have given £250.

16 Radical Theatre in an Enterprise Culture

John McGrath

Until recently, we liberals and wets in the UK regarded censorship in the Soviet Union as evidence of a monolithic, mind-controlling, paranoid regime.

But our own censorship, our own methods of repression, are not visible to the naked eye. To them, we are blind.

At the moment, we in Western Europe think we are more affluent than those in Eastern Europe. We have as consumers an immense range of choice – if we have the cash! The problem in Eastern Europe has been the much more basic one of production and distribution. But recently things have been changing. In the East, and in the West.

There is no rule that relates freedom of speech to consumerism, but simultaneously with the possibility of wider choices in the shops has come, in the Soviet Union, an opening of doors in the intellectual emporium, the creation of a new Harrods of the imagination.

We have all felt the excitement – exemplified by the two conferences on *glasnost* in Edinburgh – that Soviet writers and those involved in theatre, music, dance and film have been generating recently. The discussions at the 1987 Edinburgh Festival were on a completely different level of openness from anything experienced from the USSR since the late 1920s.

But what is happening in the West?

The polarisation in our consumer society in Britain is exemplified in our cultural life too. In our Centres of Excellence, Covent Garden, the Barbican and the National Theatre, and their satellite centres of excellence in the North, the cultural equivalent of the trim little Porsches and managerial Mercedes ooze across the stages, all much the same but with a range of bodypaint to choose from ...

And meanwhile, in the housing estates of Yorkshire, the industrial towns of Lancashire, in Edinburgh's Pilton or Glasgow's Easterhouse, the working-class areas of Birmingham, Coventry and Hackney, the fare is systematically being starved of substance, of nourishment, of health. The meat for the imagination of the mass of the population has been cynically replaced with beef-flavoured crisps by the policies of the Arts Council of Great Britain.

At the same time they have pumped such funds as they have into wonderfully rich consumerables for the Barbican-goer, and their provincial emulators, and have removed from the working class the little entertainment that respected their lives and their imaginations.

And the worst crime is not the suppression of the companies that *did* exist, but the removal of the opportunity to work of those groups which *could* have been created ...

In this context, the English method of suppression of opposition is being built into the structure of our thinking. As the French say – we are getting '*le flic en soi*': the cop in the skull.

Richard Luce, the Arts Minister, warns the arts world:

> First, that you should accept the political and economic climate in which we now live and make the best of it, whatever your own private views about it. I suggest that such a positive attitude of mind can bring surprisingly good results.

So, if we accept the political climate, we shall have 'surprisingly good results ...' Doesn't that ring a familiar bell? An alarm bell?

Glasnost's Miles Better ...

Then he spells out his whole current philosophy:

> Freedom of expression and experimentation in the arts is of profound importance. But we cannot survive in the arts without putting ourselves to the test. The only real test of our ability to succeed is whether or not we can attract enough customers.

That is simply not true. Furthermore, it is the structural device for the suppression of unpopular truth.

What do they mean by all this PR jargon?

Firstly, they mean that art must be channelled to those who will pay most for it. This is not really class-divisive, because happily, according to a Mr Douglas Mason of the Adam Smith Institute, the working class doesn't partake of art: a 1982 government report apparently 'showed audiences for artistic events were drawn, as they always had been, almost entirely from the upper and middle classes.' He draws the philanthropic conclusion that the working class who 'do not patronise the arts' should not have to pay for concert-goers, therefore we should abolish subsidy. We should, perhaps, rest content that the rich can afford to pay and the working class will be happy to do without.

The second meaning of this grocer-shop philosophy is that those working in the arts, particularly in experimental art and things requiring 'freedom of expression', should make absolutely certain that they appeal to the largest possible number of these upper and middle-class people. In other words, *not* be experimental, and exercise only that freedom of speech which meets with the approval of the Tory consensus.

The policies I have quoted have all been enunciated since the 1987 election. They are based on lies, and class prejudice, and a scarcely-veiled desire to crush anything new, different, challenging or opposi-tional to the will of the government in power at the moment.

With policies stated as openly as these, we do not have to be Duncan Campbells to see what is going on, and that it is going to get a lot worse, if we allow it to.

It is a fact that during the coal strike of 1984, several miners who had not before been out on the picket line, went out and picketed after seeing 7:84 England's production of *Six Men of Dorset*. It is a fact that every single review of this production expressed astonish-ment at Rees-Mogg's decision to cut this company on 'artistic' grounds, and his stubborn refusal of all efforts to save it. It is a fact that tens of thousands of trades unionists in Sheffield, Liverpool, Norwich, Ipswich, Newcastle, Dorset and South Wales have seen their own history on the stage, perhaps for the first time, and have been moved by what they experienced not only to the flash of recognition, but also to the will to act – even to act politically.

Within six months of *Six Men of Dorset*, 7:84 England's subsidy was totally withdrawn making it impossible to continue. Rees-Mogg continued to tell the press it was on 'artistic' grounds. Our trades unionist on the Arts Council, Gavin Laird, confirmed this truth on TV. Two months later the Arts Council said it was 'not on artistic grounds the subsidy was withdrawn'. It was, apparently, on 'policy' grounds. Gavin Laird had no comment. 7:84 England got help from the GLC. The GLC was then abolished.

7:84 England now has no funds, no office – but an audience who still need the company, but can't afford £20 a seat, which is what it would cost with no subsidy. That voice has been silenced. I hope not forever.

Whether a work of art is improved or damaged by a direct political purpose is, rightly, a matter for lively debate. But it is a matter for some alarm when the guardians of our culture appear to have made it almost impossible for a work of art with a particular political message to be made at all. Especially when those guardians have astonishingly little actual qualification for making artistic judgments of any kind apart from their adherence to the political elite that appointed them; an elite itself incapable of inspiring any work of art, with or without a purpose. (Mrs Thatcher's *Gloriana* will take a lot of composing.)

That this is indeed what is happening will be disputed with all the deadly charm of dry Tory PR, but that it is the case is now generally wearily recognised. Wearily, since the assault on civil liberties, the bending of the highest principles of the law, the cruelty of this Government's social policy have all been painfully charted by many wise and good people, only to be oiled out of sight with a velvety sigh and a coo of ministerial reassurance. If they can get away with the Belgrano, they can get away with political theatre.

7:84 England is not the only victim. CAST, a socialist group sending out to clubs all over the country variety acts that offered something other than strip and racist comedy, had their small subvention removed. Others, like Red Ladder, were 'devolved' – thrown on the mercy of local authorities, who have minimal funds and sometimes even more political volatility and venom than the Arts Council.

Socialists, you will recall, wish to reduce all nature's variety to drab uniformity: remember Mao's uniformed millions, Stalin's monolithic architecture, the little brown clones of Ho Chi Minh?

And Tories, in case you had forgotten, love individuality, enterprise, independence of spirit. Sadly, this is as untrue in the arts as in local government.

In the theatre, the concept of national and regional 'centres of excellence' is the instrument to express the Tory longing for something to look up to. It is also neat, conveniently fundable, and good for absorbing any stray dissent.

The independent theatre companies, apart from being bureaucratically inconvenient, apt to have messy books and to give away tickets to the unemployed, were also difficult to have vetted in advance by 'responsible' people.

These companies, however, attracted a tremendous amount of new talent, who created new and vibrantly different ways of doing things. Any sane, perceptive bureaucrat who cared for the future of theatre would surely have encouraged such free, intrepid and seminal companies to grow and flourish.

But instead, the legacy of these bureaucrats of the arts is that of 'centres of excellence' – the National Theatre and the RSC, and the centripetal force of the new regional elites. They buy up the bright ideas and people of the independent companies, and put them through the mincer of their production processes, sanitise their ideology, cover them in gooey lighting, and they emerge no longer vibrant, different, startling or unique, but conformist, tame and toothless. If politics is to be allowed, it is certain to be the unedifying spectacle of left-wing writers presenting a travesty of their past allegiances, or tearing their breasts in histrionic impotence.

Until the recent appointment of Sir Alan Peacock – 'one of ours' as Mrs Thatcher would say – the situation in Scotland looked distinctly opposed to political repression in the arts, which was identified as an English disease. However with the Tory disaster in Scotland in 1987, has come the professionally-organised search-and-destroy campaign to kill off socialism North of the Border – a latter-day Rough Wooing. All areas of Scottish life are being invaded by cooing Tory appointees, the Church of Scotland even having to listen to a lecture on the Christian values of exploitation and greed from the infallible Mrs Thatcher.

Small wonder that Arts Council appointments are now rigorously scrutinised by our Viceroy Rifkind, and political 'undesirables' like Kathy Finn of the teachers' union or even Judy Steele are not allowed into any position of real importance (and the Drama Committee is still chaired by an academic with elitist views and little sympathy for popular theatre).

In this atmosphere, 7:84 Scotland could not go unchallenged for very long. In March 1988 it was given twelve months' notice of total withdrawal of revenue funding. The grounds were threefold: firstly, that the Board of Directors – formed from company members, representatives of the audience, and political supporters – was not 'objective', and should consist of people with 'business skills', that is, tycoons, lawyers and accountants, the very 'responsible' people likely to vet the company in advance. Secondly, that its administration needed improvement – true, and it was being acted upon. (Incidentally, the same criticism could have been made of the Arts Council iself!) And thirdly, the 'quality' of the work is 'variable'. And here, I fear, we come up against the prejudices and definitions of 'theatre' of the assessors – unconsciously but clearly anti-working class, elitist and snobbish to the point of nausea.

At this point 7:84 is desperately trying to take the criticisms seriously, to mend its ways and to persuade the Arts Council to rescind its notice. Whether what emerges, even if it does succeed, will be identifiable with my own theatrical practice remains to be seen. (See end note.) The reason this has come about may not appear to be direct political repression. In the case of 7:84 England, CAST and some others, it clearly was. The confusion, self-contradiction and mendacity of their fictional 'reasons' for cutting 7:84 England have convinced anybody who has studied them that the real reason is political distaste, and consequent repression. The distaste is for class politics. Class, after all has been proved, to the sure satisfaction of 105 Piccadilly, not to exist. And theatre that supports working-class aspirations, and reminds people of their history and their human potential, is clearly a bit of a bore. In 1984. In Piccadilly. And on the Drama Committee of the Scottish Arts Council.

But the reason for the urge to centralisation and guaranteeable excellence is, though closely connected, due to a deeper malaise of the 1980s: the growth of the corporate-state mentality in general, and its grip on the minds of arts bureaucrats and their committees in particular.

And as this mentality oozes over our whole nation, and all the frantic warnings of the perceptive and the desperate cries of the victims are simply PR problems – to be smiled at compassionately and softly-spoken out of existence, the need for more and more theatre that can bring people together to give voice to our condition, and even move those people to take action against it, grows urgent. That it is to be frustrated by the unscrupulous actions of appointees of this government, and of a bureaucracy now lead by a buddy of the corporations, simply makes the need, and the offence against civilised values, the greater.

As we allow the now fashionable profit motive to drive us into the corporate state, soon the multinational corporate state, and the values of the market place dominate our artistic and intellectual life, this new, insidious and ultra-powerful control over the flow of information and the provision of oppositional artistic experience to the population forces us to demand not only that the scandals be brought to light, but also that the basic attitudes buried deep in the policies of this government be identified as the true enemy of humanity.

Note

On 21 July 1988 John McGrath decided that the demands and theatrical values of the Scottish Arts Council were no longer compatible with his theatrical practice and resigned as Artistic Director of 7:84 Scotland.

Postscript

Censorship has increased, is increasing ... and is now accelerating:

Even since these essays were written the following has happened:

THE BROADCASTING BAN (SINN FEIN, UDA, etc.)

Because the extent of the ban is vague and unclear it means an increase in self-censorship – when broadcasters are not sure what is permissible they err on the side of caution. Sinn Fein, for example, remains a legal organisation and can participate in other elements of democracy such as elections. As a Sinn Fein representative, Gerry Adams could therefore speak in Parliament – and be reported on radio, television and in the press. But he cannot be directly cross-examined on radio or television in defence of terrorism. Ironically he could be interviewed as an individual about increases in pensions, wages for nurses, water pollution or nursery provision and therefore emerge *only* as a caring, gentle figure! This is not a simple question of denying freedom of expression to Sinn Fein. The crucial point is that it is a denial of freedom to the British people, on a desperately important issue, to make an unimpeded and first-hand judgment on *all* the evidence. It is we who are being censored.

END OF THE RIGHT TO SILENCE

Bizarre as it may seem, within 24 hours of the Government imposing a broadcast silence they removed a general right to it in court. Starting in Northern Ireland, it is to be extended to England and Wales. The Royal Commission on Criminal Procedure in January 1981 declared that a suspect should not be obliged to answer questions and that the 'right of silence' should not be modified:

> The so-called right of silence is, in fact, another way of stating the common law principle that no man can be required (that is compelled) to incriminate himself.

The right to freedom of speech of the individual must contain within itself the right to choose when to exercise that freedom and is therefore an essential concomitant to it. However ultimately qualified, and however strongly some will defend it in the light of the exceptional circumstances of Northern Ireland, the ending of this right is a dangerous innovation in our law. Among other things it seriously erodes the hitherto carefully guarded and properly cherished balance between the requirements of the law and of freedom.

DEATH ON THE ROCK

The verdict of the inquest held in Gibraltar was one of lawful killing. No formal inquiry was held by government or parliamentary committee into the events themselves. No explanation has been given for the contradiction in various reports – for example, whether the IRA members had been under permanent supervision up to the Spanish/Gibraltar border, or why ministerial statements for 24 hours after the incident were wrong in referring to the existence and defusing of a car bomb. Yet it is widely believed that a Cabinet sub-committee was established in order to discredit the *Death on the Rock* programme. Under sharp government pressure Thames Television felt compelled to take the unique step of setting up an inquiry, under Lord Windlesham, into the accuracy of their own programme. So an inquiry was held after all – not into the event but into a television programme on the event. But there have been no such inquiries established either into the accuracy or source of initial press reports or into the initial government contradictions.

THE LOBBY

Towards the end of 1988 two events brought the lobby system of unattributable briefings into further disrepute. The first occurred when the Chancellor of the Exchequer, Nigel Lawson, 'unattributably' briefed journalists about increased means testing for pensioners; midway through, the briefing changed to 'attributable'; an hour later it had reverted to its former 'unattributable' status; the next day the Chancellor claimed that ten journalists with identical stories were in error; the journalists sought proof from the tape recorder which they had seen running throughout the briefing; they were then told the tape recorder had, unfortunately, malfunctioned! The second event occurred two weeks later when the Prime Minister, in the form of No. 10's Press Officer, sought to prevent the Queen from visiting Moscow. In an attempt to head off the expected invitation from Gorbachev Mr Bernard Ingham indicated that the Prime Minister would veto such a visit. Both cases have certain similarities: their purpose was clearly to influence events; kites were flown; apparently accurate newspaper reporting was later strenuously denied. It would be a fortunate result of these events if the rest of the media were now to follow the example of the *Guardian* and the *Independent* in refusing to participate in what has increasingly become a manipulation of news by Government.

SPYCATCHER AND THE SECRECY ACTS

By the Lords' judgement on *Spycatcher* on 13 October 1988 the British news media were finally allowed to report and comment on the contents of the book. The Lords rejected the government two-year-long argument that the duty of confidence was absolute and recognised that a public interest defence exists. Further, they unanimously stated that the government must show that publication of information would be harmful to the public interest *before* the courts would order an injunction. English common law recognises that, as Lord Goff said, 'in a free society there is a continuing public interest that the working of government should be open to scrutiny and criticism'. It was hoped that the Home Secretary would take this on board, though it was clearly counter to his proposals in the White Paper on Secrecy Reform. However, Douglas Hurd rejected the Law Lords' advice and made clear that the public interest defence would not be included in the Official Secrets Bill because, he said, 'we believe in the absolute extent of confidentiality'. (*Hansard*, 23.11.1988) So, where a civil servant reveals serious crime or corruption he or she will have no defence in law, and it is he or she who would be sent to jail. Ponting could not have been acquitted.

The allegations publicised in the Wright/*Spycatcher* case also led to a demand for, and an expectation of, democratic supervision of MI5. Though the position of MI5 has now for the first time been framed in statutory form in the Security Service Bill, the oversight and supervision remains solely in the hands of ministers, who themselves are bound by secrecy. Unlike other Western democracies there is no democratic or parliamentary oversight through a Select Committee, for example. The replacement of the past Directive by a formal and statutory definition in the Bill is of itself a dangerous extension of unregulated power. It makes potentially legal that which was illegal – for example 'bugging and burgling'. The designation of 'actions' which might 'undermine parliamentary democracy' will be left to political ministers. This is especially serious when the definition of 'actions' includes both 'political' and 'industrial', and when we have a Prime Minister who in the past has identified miners taking industrial actions as 'the enemy within'.

WHITE PAPER ON BROADCASTING

This long-awaited document is worse than anticipated. The new technologies could have given an unrivalled opportunity to expand and enrich the human experience by offering untrammelled access to a wide diversity of programme and opinion. Instead the White Paper is confined within the crippling exigencies of the market economy. It proposes that existing and future terrestrial services should be pushed towards subscription funding. There is a certain irony here since all this originated from those who argued for 'free' television and an 'end to the licence fee', yet a recent defence of subscription broadcasting claimed that 'specialist' services such as 'children's programmes, sports, film coverage, minority languages', could be provided for 'no more than £10 to £20 per month' – i.e. between double and quadruple the present licence fee!

Hitherto broadcasting in Britain has been based upon the concept of public service, encapsulated in the duty to 'inform, educate and entertain'. This applied to both the BBC and the commercial sector. Regulation ensured universality of access to programmes, maintained standards and guaranteed diversity of programme and opinion. The White Paper endangers all these. Franchises will be sold to the highest bidder. The IBA is abolished and the new Independent Television Commission (ITC) will operate with a 'lighter touch'. Positive regulation to ensure high standards will be diminished or abolished. It will instead be replaced by a system of negative controls to prevent what they call 'good taste and decency' from being offended. There is a world of difference.

The compelled move towards subscription for both the BBC and the commercial channels will, by definition, end freedom of access to all programmes. While the White Paper will ensure a proliferation of channels it will also inevitably lead to an effective diminution of real choice of programme.

The special nature of Channel 4 is also threatened. The arm's-length policy in relation to its funding has enabled it to maintain high standards and innovative, experimental and minority programmes. The White Paper says it must now compete with the other commercial channels for its funding. It is hard to see how under these requirements Channel 4's special role could survive.

The deliberate rejection by the Government of this opportunity to use the real potential of the new technologies for opening up and expanding access to new areas of knowledge and expression must be seen as one of the saddest and most dangerous attacks upon the freedom of the word in recent times. The narrowing of choice along with an increasing concentration of ownership stretching across both the written and the spoken word has serious implications for the free and open dissemination of balanced information and views.

Many freedoms have been lost in this divided society. But of these the one that must be cherished most and fought for and found again is the freedom of the word. It is always the first freedom to come under attack. It is always the first freedom to unlock the doors for all other freedoms. As Milton said:

> For this is not the liberty which we can hope, that no grievance ever should arise in the Commonwealth – that let no man in this world expect; but when complaints are freely heard, deeply considered and speedily reformed then is the utmost bound of civil liberty attained that wise men look for. (*Areopagitica*)

NORMAN BUCHAN
TRICIA SUMNER

Index